ENDOR

Well done Steve for calling all of us
and adventure of bringing Kingdom power and love into the desperate
needs of needy people. That's what I want to give my life to!

John Arnott
Catch the Fire, Toronto

"Look at the nations and watch – and be utterly amazed. For I am going
to do something in your days that you would not believe, even if you were
told" (Hab. 1:5 NIV).

Steve Stewart is a history maker and world changer! *When Everything*
Changes is an invitation to the twenty-first century slugfest Holy Spirit
is causing in the world today. Warning: The Mission Virus is contagious!
Let your heart be stirred by the things that break His heart!

Leif Hetland
President and Founder, Global Mission Awareness
Author – Seeing Through Heaven's Eyes

'The coming of the Kingdom of God' is a subject that's been debated by
theologians for centuries. Steve Stewart's ministry is based upon it. In
very practical ways he demonstrates that God's Kingdom can be really
experienced by men and women everywhere. This book encourages us
that when the people of God faithfully practice the principles of God then
the Lord shows up. And a foretaste of Heaven is experienced here on earth.

Peter Kerridge
CEO, Premier Christian Media
London, UK

Steve Stewart has done it. Don't read this book unless you are ready to
have your mind blown and your calendar wrecked. *When Everything*
Changes will make you rethink life and it won't let you go until you
reorder your own. Steve Stewart takes us on a journey of compassion
that gets us off the couch and into the battle.

Alan Hawkins
Founder, New Life City Network

Steve Stewart has delivered a book that ignites a fire in the heart of the believer for seeing the Kingdom of God manifested in the earth today. A powerful and practical read for those who desire to do the greater works of Jesus, but have lacked the tools to live it out on a daily basis. Put this book into practice and it will radically transform your world!

John D. Mullen
National Director, Believer's Edge, USA

When Everything Changes comes at a time when the Church needs to revise our approach to reaching the lost, from a Church mindset to a Kingdom mindset! I believe this book is here for this purpose: "To help the reader occupy until Christ returns." As you read it, remember it comes not only from the inspiration of the Holy Spirit, but too, from a long-lived experience of Church dynamics that Steve has grown through!

Robert Mponye
Founding Pastor
King's Kid Ministries International, Uganda

I have known and ministered with Steve Stewart for 12 years and I deeply appreciate the man, the ministry and the message. Steve pursues passionately and longs for ever-increasing measures of the Kingdom with childlike abandon that obviously delights the Father's heart as much as it transforms us. This book will make readers reach out and experience a joyful, exuberant call to action and a downloading of Kingdom authority! Be warned.

Bob Brasset,
Kingdom Advancers, Victoria, BC, Canada

We know Pastor Steve and Christina personally and are so proud to be part of Impact Nations. We are witnesses to his passion for Kingdom expansion and the outbreak of physical, spiritual and emotional healing in our country. In his book, *When Everything Changes*, Pastor Steve explores a person's deepest hidden need and cry for the Kingdom of God, healing and justice.

Vijay & Neeraja Christian
Founder, Friends Meet Ministries
Vishakhapatnam, India

WHEN EVERYTHING CHANGES

HEALING, JUSTICE AND THE KINGDOM OF GOD

STEVE STEWART

WHEN EVERYTHING CHANGES:
HEALING, JUSTICE AND THE KINGDOM OF GOD

ESV	English Standard Version
GWT	God's Word Translation
KJV	King James Version
NKJV	New King James Version
NCV	New Century Version
CEV	Contemporary English Version
NLT	New Living Translation
TLB	The Living Bible
MSG	The Message
RSV	Revised Standard Version
NRSV	New Revised Standard Version
NASB	New American Standard Bible
TNIV	Today's New International Version

To contact the author or order copies, visit www.impactnations.org

ISBN: 978-0-99811409-5-7

**Library Archives of Canada Cataloguing in Publication
available on request**

Fresh Wind Press
2170 Maywood Crt.,
Abbotsford, BC Canada V2S 4Z1

DEDICATION

To Christina:

For more than forty years you have loved me, believed in me and stayed by my side through this great adventure, even when it got uncertain and frightening. Thank you for your lifelong example of steadfast faithfulness to our Lord. Thank you for all that you have poured into our children, and now our grandchildren. Thank you for following me across this country and to nations around the world. Thank you for stepping out from what you know and are comfortable with for the sake of Jesus. You are my greatest friend on this earth. You are my joy. I will always love you.

TABLE OF CONTENTS

FOREWORD
RANDY CLARK

Steve Stewart is one of the persons that heaven would call "the Friend of God." I say this because I believe Steve has a heart for God and for the things on God's heart. I have known him for seventeen years. He was one of the first pastors to come to the outpouring in Toronto in January 1994. He and his church were tremendously touched. I used to tell about Steve having to stay home for days due to being so touched he shook, fell and stuttered when he spoke. Steve was one of the most successful church planters in the early Vineyard movement, one of the best preachers. But, God had touched him, including his great gift of speaking, to test him. Steve passed the test; he cherished the experience of being touched by God, even when it had this humbling temporary experience of stuttering. This book reflects the fruit of this touch of God, and I might add it is tremendous fruit.

Years later I met Steve again, we became friends, and he traveled with me to several countries. For a while our ministries worked together in a cooperative effort called GAIN (Global Awakening–Impact Nations) to minister to the widows and orphans, and provide water treatment for villages in India. This is where I saw Steve Stewart's heart for God and for the special concerns that are on God's heart; concerns for the poor, the widow and the orphan; concerns for His Church to be in revival, His people to be renewed; concerns for the Kingdom to be expressed through His people, especially in healing and deliverance, as well as its ministry to the marginalized people.

In *When Everything Changes* you too will be able to see the heart of a man who loves God, and is loved by God, expressed in powerful concepts, written with passion and wisdom. This book reveals Steve's solid commitment to the Bible, and his solid commitment that Christians, the Church, and Christianity should emphasize what the Bible emphasizes; for example, the Kingdom, healing, and justice. His book is divided into three parts that reflect this emphasis of God's heart and the Bible.

Section one, The Kingdom of God, discusses the nature of the King and his Kingdom, how the Kingdom is released, and compassion as the motive of the Kingdom. Section two, Healing, discusses healing as the manifestation of the Kingdom, keys to increase healing, and a simple healing model. Section three, Justice, discusses justice and the Kingdom, the role of the Church, and the revolutionary gospel.

Steve has written an amazing book. I am so happy to see someone who is an evangelical write a book that has an emphasis upon justice. This, in my opinion, makes this book extremely important for Christian leaders to read. I believe the charismatic world that has so much emphasis upon personal prophecy, and the evangelical world that has an emphasis upon end-time prophecy, needs to have the plumb line of God's word to bring back the biblical concern of prophecy for the poor, the widow and orphan, and for justice. I am glad to see the prophetic spirit in, *When Everything Changes*, powerfully expressed through Steve's writing.

The gospel had the emphasis of both personal and social dimensions in its presentation until the 1920's–30's Modernist–Fundamentalist Controversy. As a result of this controversy the Fundamentalists and Evangelicals focused primarily on the personal dimension of salvation, while the Liberals focused on the social dimension almost entirely. In this way the gospel itself was distorted, God's word doesn't allow us an either/or choice, it demands a both/and position to be the authentic gospel. Steve has recaptured part of the gospel that many conservatives have failed to emphasize.

But, it isn't just the biblical emphasis of justice that Steve re-emphasizes; the Kingdom, and healing are also major emphases of the Bible. This book captures the heart of God. I highly recommend *When Everything Changes* to all pastors, leaders and disciples of Jesus. I further want to take this opportunity to highly recommend Steve Stewart and his ministry to you as well

Randy Clark

PREFACE TO THE SECOND EDITION

It has been three years since *When Everything Changes* was first released. To my surprise and delight, people have kindly written from many places in the world, telling me that it has been insightful and helpful in their journey.

Occasionally, I am asked why I wrote this book. One issue I wanted to address is the discrepancy between two fairly distinct groups in the church, those who see our task as primarily to proclaim the need for people to come to faith in Jesus Christ, this being the central point of the Gospel, and those who believe that it is more important to bring social change in the name of Jesus. Too often, this has led to a divide in the purpose and goal of urban and overseas missions, and in the essential message of the church.

For many years, I have been convinced that the Gospel which Jesus, the disciples and the early church proclaimed was big enough to touch all areas of life. If, as I believe, Jesus is the only way to know abundant and eternal life (John 17:3), then the Gospel *must* be preached to all people, in all nations. (And I believe this is most effectively done when proclamation is accompanied by supernatural demonstrations of healing.) But I am equally persuaded that when we feed the hungry and provide clean water, medicine and employment opportunities to the poor, not only are we demonstrating the Gospel, but according to Matthew 25:31-40, we are actually ministering *to* Jesus. These two views of the Gospel are not contradictory; they are mutually supportive and dependent upon one another.

My second reason for writing *When Everything Changes* is somewhat paradoxical. With all my heart, I believe that there has been too much talking about the Gospel and too little living it out. Frankly, we don't have trouble believing who Jesus is; our problem is with fully believing what He said. And He said that if we want to build our lives on a solid foundation, we have to put His words into action. And here is the paradox: by writing a book that calls for an active, inclusive, all-reaching Gospel, I am adding to the word pile. I just hope that what I have to say will somehow encourage people to move from concept to practice.

It is my prayer that *When Everything Changes* will encourage, challenge and equip all those who pursue the adventure of following Jesus.

1

WHEN EVERYTHING CHANGES

And the one sitting on the throne said, "Look, I am making everything new!"   REVELATION 21:5 NLT

It was another warm and clear day in southern India, typical for the winter months. I was in a village of about fifteen thousand with a team of forty-five people who had gathered from several nations. After spending some time together worshiping and praying, we went out with more excitement than apprehension, looking forward to what Jesus was going to do that day.

We had set up a mobile clinic in a Muslim community that had never had anything like this happen before. In no time hundreds of people had gathered to receive medical care and, for those who wanted it, the offer of prayer. Partway into the morning I took some team members out into the village so that they could see more of village life and have opportunity to pray for the sick – and there were many, many opportunities. As soon as the first couple of people were healed, villagers seemed to come from everywhere. It is always this way when the Kingdom comes.

After some time I went back to the mobile clinic in order to get a few more team members and take them out to the village. On the edge of the clinic was a table with a group of girls laughing and talking and enjoying the crayons and coloring books that team members had brought. For some reason this happy group of children caught my attention. As I walked through the clinic, where there were a couple of hundred people who were waiting to be seen, there was an air of excitement, an atmosphere very different from when I had left an hour earlier. A team member immediately beckoned me over to meet the Muslim chief of the village. People all around were very excited to tell me what had happened in my absence.

A Muslim lady had brought in her seven-year-old daughter for medical treatment. She told one of our medical team that her daughter had been born completely deaf and therefore also had never spoken. The woman had brought the girl to get some medicine to help cure this problem. Our team member looked at the woman and told her, "I am sorry, but there is no medicine anywhere that will heal your daughter's problem. But I will pray for her and Jesus will heal her." Placing her hands on the girl's ears she commanded, in the name of Jesus, the deafness to leave; the girl's eyes became wide and she started to look around. The team member, realizing what was happening, spontaneously exclaimed, "Oh God, you are so good!" Immediately the little girl repeated in perfect English, "Oh God, you are so good." Her mother started speaking to her daughter in their native language, Telagu, and with no hesitation or difficulty her daughter began to speak back to her.

How could this happen? How could a girl who had never heard a sound instantly speak and make herself understood? Only Jesus could do this. After telling me this, they turned and pointed out the little girl to me; she was one of those girls happily talking and coloring at the table.

At this point the Muslim chief pulled me aside and through a translator said, "That was amazing! I have never seen anything like it." He then told me how twenty-two years earlier he had an accident and ever since then he suffered serious back pain, which in fact had been recently exacerbated and was causing him a great deal of discomfort. He asked me, "Do you think that Jesus would heal me too?" After assuring him that Jesus loves to heal, I quietly and discreetly put my hand on his back and commanded the pain to go. His look of amazement told me all I needed to know, and then his words confirmed that all of his pain was gone. This Muslim chief followed us for the next three days as we did mobile clinics in different communities nearby. In each of these communities he seemed to know people who needed healing and would bring them to me, simply announcing, "Jesus needs to heal this one, too." And again and again, Jesus did exactly that.

The ending to this story did not come for several more months. The Muslim chief and some of his other leaders came for the first time ever and talked with our partners who were ministering in that area. After thanking them once again for bringing Impact Nations to their Muslim community, the chief announced that they had a piece of land adjacent to our partner's property that they wanted to give to them in appreciation so that a small permanent clinic could be built. The clinic was built and now offers treatment to the surrounding community.

•   •   •

When the Kingdom of God comes with the power and reality of heaven, everything begins to change. The possibilities change, the scope of our dreams and hopes changes, and lives are profoundly transformed. The Kingdom of God is bigger, more immediate, more powerful, more inclusive than most of us have ever imagined. The gospel of the Kingdom that Jesus preached and demonstrated, this gospel that He entrusted to His disciples and to the church, is meant to touch everything. The gospel of the Kingdom is unshakable and irresistible. Jesus declared that it is forcefully advancing and He challenged us to take hold of its forcefulness. The gospel of the Kingdom is why we as Jesus' disciples are here. It is the great adventure. It is the ultimate purpose of life. The Kingdom has a King and He is moving; He says, "Follow Me. Look where I'm going. Join in what I am doing."

We have largely settled for a gospel that is safe and staid, a gospel that does not stir fire in the hearts of those who hear it. Is *this* the gospel of the Kingdom that the disciples and the early church preached everywhere? Is *this* the gospel for which men and women gladly gave their lives?

The radical transformational gospel that the early church proclaimed confronted the powers of the age, and it changed history. The Kingdom comes to transform lives at every level – individually and corporately – economically, socially, supernaturally. It is a gospel of rescue. It is the gospel of confrontation against injustice. It is the gospel that is demonstratively good news to the poor. It is the gospel that confronts the *status quo*. It is a gospel that brings transformation wherever it is embraced.

For too long we have preached too small and too tame a gospel, a gospel that has essentially told people to go to church, be nice, and wait for heaven where everything will sort itself out. But the gospel that Jesus preached, the gospel that confronted nations, the gospel that led to martyrdom for almost all of the twelve disciples – this is not, and never was a polite and safe gospel.

THE GREATER STORY

We are created for significance. Even more, we are created for adventure. This is because God has made us to participate in His Greater Story – His eternal and ever-unfolding plan for His creation. We are created to be part of that plan and in this we find our deepest satisfaction. This is why from the youngest age we are drawn to stories of heroism, of great causes. By the time my grandson was three years old he was enthralled with heroes. (When I open the front door I never know which superhero will be greeting me!) And we never really outgrow this. The heroes that we follow in books and on the movie screen - all touch something very deep within us. These are merely a shadow, an expression of the desire that is in every person to participate in something that has significance beyond one's self. I believe that when beckoned, the disciples followed Jesus not only because He looked into their hearts with compassion and understanding, but also they recognized an invitation to a greater cause.

One of the early church fathers, Iranaeus, said, "The Glory of God is man fully alive." Life is a great gift and a great adventure which, when fully embraced, not only brings us a tremendous sense of fulfillment, but also advances the purposes of God and His Kingdom upon the earth. It is our adversary who continually tries to restrain us through fear and intimidation. Our enemy wants us to think small thoughts, to dream small dreams. We are surrounded by a culture that continually sends out the message to "settle down" and settle for less.

King David understood what it was to face fear and intimidation and yet, to prevail. At the end of his reign he passed the torch to his son Solomon, commissioning him to the almost overwhelming task of building a great temple for the Lord. Knowing the challenges that Solomon would be facing, David said this to his son: *"Be strong and courageous and do it. Do not be afraid and do not be dismayed, for the Lord God, even my God, is with you. He will not leave you or forsake you until all the work for the service of the house of the Lord is finished"* (1 Chr. 28:20).

There is a Zulu word my friends and I like to use to encourage each other: *Vukani*. It means, "Get up and do something!" Every one of us needs a community of friends, of disciples who will strengthen and encourage us to keep going as we pursue the cause of Christ. The writer to the Hebrews knew the power of this when he said, *"Let us consider how to stir up one another to love and good works"* (Heb. 10:24). These communities of disciples are more than places of nurture and encouragement; they are also launching pads that send out men and women to the nations.

I have the privilege of working with some very heroic men

and women around the world. They live in a great diversity of situations in Asia, Africa and Central America; yet they have this in common: a passion for Christ and His gospel which is lived out through radical obedience to Him:

A group of pastors and their families in Manila move into Payatas, the largest garbage dump in the Philippines, in order to reach and care for the poorest, most desperate people in their city. They live in squalor in a community of over one hundred thousand for the sake of the Gospel. Some of them have now been there for over twenty years. Their commitment to helping and encouraging one another is unwavering. And the Kingdom steadily advances in Payatas.

An ex-gang member lives with his family in a squatters' village in Nicaragua. Daily he cares for this poor settlement, helping them to get food, praying for the sick, building shelters and the makeshift school. And slowly, the village is being transformed through the obedience of this man and his family.

A young pastor in Haiti leads a church of new believers, most of them coming to Christ just after the 2010 earthquake. They live in the poverty of ninety-five percent unemployment, as he teaches them that in the new community of Jesus, *"No one claimed that any of his possessions was his own, but they shared everything they had"* (Acts 4:32). With this understanding, they regularly walk for hours to care for and help others in the mountains. This culture of following Jesus wherever He takes them is leading them to more and more communities in Haiti, bringing hope in the midst of the devastation that continues to wreak havoc in this shattered nation.

A young couple in India forsake the opportunity for economic and social advancement that their education and training could make available to them. Instead they give themselves to taking the gospel to rural villages both near and far, and to the wretchedly poor in their own city. And, as so often happens, their passion for Christ is a fire that draws other young men and women to them.

And now a community of disciples, radically obedient to the cause of God's Kingdom has emerged. And wherever they go, men, women and children turn to Jesus.

Where God is moving in revival there is always radical obedience. This kind of radical commitment truly amazes us, and at one level it should. But at another level, it is this kind of immediate response to Jesus' invitation that marked the early church. After all, its first members set the standard:

> *"Come, follow me," Jesus said, "and I will make you fishers of men." At once they left their nets and followed him. Going on from there, he saw two other brothers, James son of Zebedee and his brother John. They were in a boat with their father Zebedee, preparing their nets. Jesus called them, and immediately they left the boat and their father and followed him* (Matt. 4:19–22).

JESUS' INVITATION

This is a time of unprecedented opportunity. I am watching God raise up people who are completely committed to bringing His Kingdom to the poor and the hurting of the world. And wherever these passionate disciples go, they release the tangible signs of God's Kingdom, bringing healing, hope, justice and rescue. Everywhere I go within the church or outside of it, I encounter people who are longing for more significance, more purpose. They are beginning to gather.

The inclusive Jesus continues to say, "You come too. Of course this is for you!" I see young men and women not content with simply wishing that there were more to their lives, but stepping out and following Jesus into the harvest field, becoming actively engaged in His Greater Story. I see young families willing to leave conventional security in order to find their security in Christ. I see men and women who traditionally would be moving into the quiet life of retirement but instead have heard the Master's call to come follow Him where He is going. These are men and women who do not see themselves disqualified by their age, who long to run the race hard to the end. I agree with Jim Wallis who wrote, "Our churches are meant to be dynamic counter-cultural communities whose purpose is to re-shape old lives and societies."[1]

There is something profoundly counter-cultural that is going on; men and women are stepping away in growing numbers from the *status quo*. They are discovering the adventure, the challenge and the joy of embracing Jesus words, *"If anyone would come after Me, let him deny himself and take up his cross and follow Me. For whoever would save his life will lose it, but whoever loses his life for My sake will find it"* (Matt. 16: 24–25).

I have the privilege to be surrounded by people like this. In January 2010, Adam went to Haiti to preach the gospel and to see healing released. A few days after he arrived, a massive earthquake struck, killing over three hundred thousand Haitians in under a minute. In fact, he was there with my wife Christina, preparing for a future Journey of Compassion. After two long and chaotic days filled with much difficulty and danger, they were able to fly out of the country. As soon as Adam was home he began to gather funds and share the need with anyone who would listen. He then immediately got on a plane for the Dominican Republic. From there he joined with a pastor and they drove a bus to Haiti filled with medicine and food. No red tape. No complications. No delay. Since then Adam has gone again and again, sometimes on his own and sometimes bringing others with him. He has seen thousands of Haitians healed and give their lives to Jesus. He has also facilitated medical care and feeding. Adam knows that good news for the poor includes both the proclamation and the practical demonstration of the Kingdom of God. A fire, which I am watching burn ever hotter, has been ignited in the hearts of this young man and his wife.

---

1 Jim Wallis, *God's Politics* (New York: HarperCollins, 2005), 7.

There are too many stories to tell – about people like Gowry, a semi-retired nurse who was grieving the death of her husband four years ago when a friend encouraged her to come on a Journey of Compassion to India. Gowry went but with trepidation, still carrying a deep sadness. But as she gave her life away in medical clinics and praying for the sick in the villages, a fire was ignited in her, too. Since then she has traveled every few months around the developing world, always going to the most needy and often the most distant.

Heidi and Kate, two nurses that have traveled with us from the beginning, recognized the opportunity to work even more effectively in remote villages by going back to university for two years of graduate training. Not only did this cost them time from being out in the field where their passions lay, it meant intensive study at a cost of many tens of thousands of dollars. So why did they do this? They had heard Jesus call them to get prepared to follow Him to some of the sickest rural communities in the world.

I also see those who, passionate for the Greater Story, are called to keep the supply lines open so that others may keep moving forward. These are those who make lifestyle decisions in order to provide for others. These are those who delight in following the apostle John's directive to his friend Gaius when he wrote:

"You will do well to send them on their journey in a manner worthy of God for they have gone out for the sake of the Name, accepting nothing from the Gentiles. Therefore we ought to support people like these, that we may be fellow workers for the truth" (3 John 6–8 ESV).

A TIME FOR BIGGER DREAMS

The scope and the urgency of God's Greater Story is calling people up, to believe for more and dream for more than ever before. His great cause enlarges hearts. This is a time for enlargement, a time for our hearts and vision to catch up with the forceful advancement of the kingdom of God. Enlargement is a powerful prophetic theme in the Scripture: the book of Acts is about enlargement. The book of Genesis is about enlargement. The prophet Isaiah wrote this:

> *Enlarge the place of your tent,*
> *stretch your tent curtains wide,*
> *do not hold back; lengthen your cords,*
> *strengthen your stakes.*
> *For you will spread out to the right and to the left;*
> *your descendants will dispossess nations*
> *and settle in their desolate cities.*
> *Do not be afraid; you will not be put to shame.*
> *Do not fear disgrace; you will not be humiliated.*
> (Isa. 54:2–4)

In the original language enlarge means literally to open wide, to make room for. This passage is an invitation for us to make changes, for us to make room for the gospel of the Kingdom in our hearts and not to wait for God to change us. Likewise, we are to take the initiative to stretch and not to hold back, to lengthen our cords and strengthen our stakes. This is a call for us to be proactive, to be forcefully advancing (Matt. 11:12). And when we make room for God to do something new in our lives, He responds to our obedience and begins to spread us out, to increase our influence and our effectiveness.

This passage brings us the promise of increase through sons and daughters. This is a very important point. Those who are enlarging – those who have stepped out in pursuit of what Jesus is doing – always attract spiritual sons and daughters. This takes us back to Hebrews 10:24, because God calls us not only to go but also to encourage others along the way. John Wesley was right – people will gather around the passion of a man or woman. As soon as you give yourself to the nations, be prepared for spiritual sons and daughters to be gathered to you (which of course brings a whole new set of challenges and delights!).

In this passage we see that God is a realist: If we step out, we step into a battle. In John 10:10 Jesus told us that there is a thief who constantly lies and tries to steal from us. The primary way he does this is through fear. Fear can be such a pervasive force that when we give in to it long enough it becomes complacency. The enemy tells us that if we step out we will suffer shame, disgrace and humiliation. These reflect a deep-seated fear of abandonment that is primal for most people. But he is the father of lies. Our true Father tells us that He will never leave us or abandon us, that He will be with us. More than that, He will empower and enable us to complete the assignment that He sets before us.

There is a certain irony that although we in the West pursue vicarious adventure through entertainment, we are reluctant to speak in large terms. Although we in the church should be the most vocal in calling people up to a great purpose, the great adventure of living in the Kingdom Of God, we settle for small things in this present age. We put our desires and hopes off into the Age to Come. With over half the world suffering in extreme poverty, with more slaves living now than at any time in history, there has never been a greater need for men and women to rise up and activate their faith. Surely creation is groaning in longing and anticipation, waiting for the children of God to make themselves known (Rom. 8:19). Never in all of history have there been such opportunities to affect change in the farthest corners of the earth as we experience today. The transportation, communication, and technological advances make possible today what could only be dreamed of a generation ago.

People who begin to activate their faith and desires can always make a greater difference, and more quickly, than they ever thought possible. This discovery awakens something deep within us when we find out that the desires of our heart are not fantasies, but a reflection of our Father's desire and intent for us. As I have simply made a way for men and women from around the world to engage in hands-on ministry among the poor, the sick and the oppressed, again and again I have watched as they have come alive. When Jesus sent out the twelve disciples and later the seventy-two, they returned with great joy. Why? Because they were doing what God had created them to do. They were moving in the rhythm of His Kingdom.

Disciples of Jesus have discovered a great cause and they are unafraid to give themselves fully to it. In many ways disciples live bigger lives, not because of who *they* are but because of who *Jesus* is. Disciples walk in spiritual authority, which has been described as *confidence without arrogance; humility without apology*. John Wesley once said that people will come for miles around to watch a man burn. He meant burn with passion and purpose. Disciples are willing to live large lives: lives that encourage and inspire others; lives that challenge the status quo; lives that are willing to be laid down for the sake of the One they are following. This is a joyful, exuberant call to action.

JOURNAL ENTRY: A SINGLE DAY IN NKWAZI, ZAMBIA

The team had been ministering together in Zambia for about a week, going into various remote villages that seem locked in time. We were very pleased to be able to bring medical care and to share the love of Jesus with these gentle people.

But on this morning we were in a very different kind of place – Nkwazi is an urban ghetto of over thirty thousand people on the outskirts of a large city. Nkwazi has the highest rate of violent crime, alcoholism and HIV/AIDS in the nation. No idyllic thatched huts here; no sounds of children laughing and playing. Instead, a cacophony of strident noise assaulted us. As the team walked through this urban ghetto, heading toward the building where we would be conducting a medical clinic, I saw and sensed rising tension among the team. Nkwazi is a jolt to the senses; as we walked through its center we sensed the atmosphere of frustration, despair and anger that hangs over this community like a blanket. Beyond the walls of the clinic we could hear the continuous sounds of shouting and frustration as the crowd pressed against the front gate.

We opened the gate and let the first hundred come in for medical treatment. Several team members moved among those waiting for treatment, offering to pray. Almost all of them immediately responded with an eager, "Yes, please." As the team prayed something began to shift; we could all feel the heaviness around this place beginning to lift. Someone was healed, and then another, and another. There was a rising excitement – some people began to clap and shout as God's healing mercy and power moved

13

like a wave through the crowd. Before the morning was over, four totally blind people were instantly and completely healed. One of them was an older lady who had been dropped off at the clinic by her twin sister. And when, an hour later, she returned and looked at her sister with eyes no longer sunken and dark but sparkling and alive she shouted and danced and cried all at once.

In the midst of this glorious God-activity, the medical staff pressed on hour after hour as the people continued to come in faster than we could treat them. In the afternoon a young man carried in his crippled father and propped him up against the wall so that the old man could receive medicine for his ailments. One of our youngest team members, emboldened by what she had seen God do all day, asked the man if she could pray for him – "Yes. Thank you." After a short prayer she asked the man to stand. Suddenly he looked upset and insulted, thinking that this young lady was mocking his crippled condition. "I can't walk!" Yet with gentleness and a new confidence, she said, "Oh sir, you couldn't walk – but now you can." Looking into his eyes she took his hand and said, "Stand up." And he did exactly that. Then he took some steps and began to walk, faster and faster. All this time his adult son kept repeating to anyone who would listen, "I don't understand. I always carry him everywhere. I don't understand."

Later that afternoon I walked through Nkwazi with my friend Jane. Almost twenty years ago she and her husband chose to move to Nkwazi and begin ministering there simply because it was the most needy place in the nation. Jane is a woman full of joy and tough as nails. We were talking at the side of a big dusty field watching a group of young men playing soccer. Suddenly, angry words were exchanged and in a few moments, at least one hundred young men converged. Jane took me by the hand and ran into the thick of it. She tried humor, reasoning, even shouting to diffuse the situation. Then in a flash, violence erupted all around us. Jane grabbed my arm and we squeezed our way out of the now flailing, kicking crowd. Back at the road, Jane told me that this is what life is like here all the time. So much time on their hands. So much frustration and poverty. Nkwazi is a tinderbox.

• • •

Six o'clock and it is beginning to get dark. The clinic is closed; the team members are tired but thrilled by what they saw the Lord do today. We are back at the sandy field in the middle of the town. It is almost deserted.

All we have are a few musicians and a very loud, but ragged PA system on the back of a small truck. A few minutes of enthusiastic singing begins to draw people to the field where only two hours ago there was such violence. I preach and Jane translates. After awhile, I give an invitation for people to turn to Jesus. Immediately some begin to come forward. But then something invisible begins to happen. The Holy presence of God begins to move through this place. It is unlike anything I have ever experienced in all the other countries, all the other outdoor meetings. I can see people hundreds of yards away who, just a moment before, were talking (as they had been while Jane & I were preaching). Suddenly they start to come toward us. From the back of the truck I can see them coming from the road, from between houses, from the main street that only a few minutes ago was loud with its raucous activity. And still they come. This is the longest appeal I ever remember giving. But they are still coming. There are tears, and there is a holy kind of silence among them.

To my left, there is a line of houses that run along the edge of the field. Now people are coming out from these houses; many of them are pushing through to be at the front of the crowd, now grown to about six hundred and fifty people. They are so close that I can see their tears and hear them crying. Without my or anyone's saying it, we know that this is a holy moment. After leading them in prayers of repentance and forgiveness, our team moves among them for an hour or more – and God is healing so many.

Later, as we drive away, joyful and thankful, and with a feeling of awe for what Jesus did in our midst, I ask Jane, "Did you notice that last group of people who came out of their houses and came right to the front?" Jane looks at me for a moment, then, begins to laugh uproariously – "Steve, those weren't houses. Those were our town brothels and bars!"

• • •

I am convinced that as we learn to move in the rhythm of God's Kingdom, He takes the little that we have to offer and multiplies it. All He is looking for is a compassionate heart and willing hands. Not great gifting, not great knowledge, just enough love to step out of the familiar to where Jesus is waiting for us.

2

HOW BIG IS THE GOSPEL OF THE KINGDOM?

Then he said, "Go into the world. Go everywhere and announce the Message of God's good news to one and all."

MARK 16:15 MSG

"There's got to be more."

I have heard those words again and again over the years. As a church planter, as a pastor, as head of a mission organization – again and again men and women share this sentiment with me. I think I know why: It is because something deep inside of us is made for something greater and that greater thing is the Kingdom of God. When that is not experienced, when it is not understood, in time our hearts move in the direction of either frustration or apathy.

Sociologists, psychologists, and theologians have all come to the same conclusion. Every man, woman and child, regardless of background, culture, or race, has been created with two great needs: security and significance. From the moment of our first breath every one of us has needed to be nurtured and protected, and to receive the identity that only comes from belonging. Also, there is a desire in every one of us for our lives to make a difference, for our lives to have an abiding significance during our time here on

17

earth.

This is reflected in two of the great themes in Scripture. In Isaiah 2 and Micah 4 we read, "Let us go up to the mountain of the Lord." In the last days there will be a great gathering of people from every nation, who become aware that God is doing something, and they do not want to miss out. They want to belong, to be in the center of this new community. Clearly this reflects the desire for security and belonging.

The second great theme is found in Ezekiel 47 and Revelation 22 where we are told that the river of God flows out from the temple. Two things stand out here: wherever the river flows it brings life, change and vitality. Secondly, the further the river goes away from the temple, the deeper it is. This vision reflects the mission of the church and provides a deep sense of significance for all of its members.

●   ●   ●

The gospel of the Kingdom is a radical, all encompassing declaration of a whole new reality. It is a gospel of restoration and of rescue, of supernatural intervention and creation, of valuing the least and the forgotten. The gospel of the Kingdom redefines family, embraces community, and engages us in the greater story. God's great purpose is His Kingdom.

George E. Ladd, who wrote extensively on the theology of the Kingdom of God, defined it as:

[T]he redemptive reign of God dynamically active to establish his rule among men, and that this Kingdom, which will appear as an apocalyptic act at the end of the age, has already come into human history in the person and mission of Jesus to overcome evil, to deliver men from its power, and to bring them into the blessings of God's reign. The Kingdom of God involves two great moments: fulfillment with history, and consummation at the end of

history.[2]

Gradually over the centuries, the Church has largely settled for too small a gospel. I am convinced that this is because we have a very real enemy who persistently seeks to reduce and neutralize the message of the gospel of the Kingdom. The result of a small gospel is small expectations, which in turn lead to apathy. Jesus proclaimed and demonstrated a gospel that was radical, powerful, and that confronted the social, economic, religious and political powers of His day. This is the gospel that men and women took to the ends of the known world at the cost of their lives. This is the gospel that, when its power and ultimate significance are understood and embraced, gives the greatest meaning to every life.

This gospel of the Kingdom, when faithfully proclaimed and demonstrated, releases the power of God and His ultimate reality in such a way that it must always bring about deep, meaningful, significant change. The gospel of the Kingdom is God's great cosmic purpose released upon the earth. The Kingdom of God touches every part of life – nothing is excluded. When a blind woman's eyes are suddenly opened; this is the Kingdom in action. When a paralyzed man stands up, when a withered hand straightens out, this is the Kingdom. But the Kingdom is also expressed when a family receives clean, safe drinking water for the first time. When anti-malarial medicine is given, this is the good news to the poor that Jesus declared. The Kingdom challenges social, economic, and political structures. It redefines reality. In fact, it releases and activates the very reality that it proclaims.

Jesus said more about the Kingdom of God than anything else He ever talked about. At various times He said the Kingdom is near, the Kingdom is close at hand, the Kingdom is among you, the Kingdom is coming, the Kingdom has come. The message of the Kingdom of God is not ethereal. It is not a concept. It is ultimate

2 George E. Ladd, *A Theology of the New Testament* (Grand Rapids: Eerdmans, 1974), 91.

reality. Jesus began His ministry by proclaiming the Kingdom, He spoke of the Kingdom more than anything else in His three and a half years of ministry, and in the forty days between His resurrection and ascension, Jesus taught His disciples about the Kingdom of God.

The New Testament calls us to live by faith. Faith believes in, and clings to the goodness, love and power of God. Faith is not a concept; authentic faith always needs to be activated. Our faith calls us to join with God in His mission: the Kingdom. As we see His mission and say yes to it, we enter into His unwavering purpose to bring about transformation here and now.

• • •

One evening I was teaching a group of believers in the church in India. The pastors, unable to get a babysitter for their nine-year-old son Abishiek, brought him to the meeting and laid him down to sleep on a bench at the back of the room. After teaching some simple healing principles to the people gathered there, I had them pray for one another using this simple model. All across the front of the church God was healing men and women. Unknown to his parents, Abishiek had been watching and listening attentively. The next afternoon he came bursting through the front door after school shouting, "It works! It works!" His friend at school had been ill for two or three days; so Abishiek asked if he could pray for the boy, then simply did what he had watched the night before. His friend was completely healed. Two days later he accompanied his father and me as we went to a fairly remote village. Abishiek begin to pray for the sick who had gathered around us. One after another was healed. Before long a man who was totally deaf stood in front of this nine-year-old boy. He too was completely healed. When word of this began to spread through the village people came out of their homes and crowds followed us as we walked through the dirt laneways. Again and again men, women and children were totally healed.

A fifty-year-old Christian woman came with us for two weeks to remote villages in the Philippines. Although this was all completely new to her, she began to pray for the sick, lead people to Jesus, and care for the poor in practical ways. A couple of weeks after her return to Canada, her husband called me and told me that he had a new wife, that she was like a completely different person.

A physician from England came with us to Central America along with her fifteen-year-old daughter. Three months later I was in their home in London when her husband stood up before a large group of their friends and neighbors and said that his wife and daughter were like different people.

What happened to all of these people? They discovered the powerful reality of the Kingdom of God.

THE KINGDOM OF GOD: VARIOUS INTERPRETATIONS

The gospel writers used different terms for describing the Kingdom. Mark and Luke wrote of the "Kingdom of God"; Matthew, who was writing to a more Jewish audience, used the term "Kingdom of Heaven." While Matthew used this term because of cultural sensitivity, I believe there is another aspect that must be considered. The literal term used by Matthew is "the Kingdom of the heavens." This term reminds us of the vastness and magnificence of God and His Kingdom. It also speaks to us of the immanence of the heavenly realm all around us, reminding us that any moment this ultimate reality of "the heavens" can break in.

Historically, there are four principal ways that the church has understood the Kingdom:

The Kingdom is synonymous with heaven. For the first several years of following Jesus, whenever I read about the Kingdom in my Bible, I automatically and unconsciously replaced the word Kingdom with heaven. This is a very common view in the church.

Jesus is speaking about our next life when we are with Him in heaven. This puts all of His Kingdom teaching into the future, describing what our life with Him will be like in heaven. With this understanding, when the church prays, "Thy Kingdom come," it is praying for the end of history, for Jesus' final coming, so that all who belong to Him may go with Him to heaven.

The church and the Kingdom are very nearly synonymous. This was a major view in the Reformation. In his writings, Martin Luther expressed his conviction that the Kingdom breaks in through the preaching of the Gospel. The focus is not so much on heaven as it is on God's bringing power for this life through His word. Very often this view of the Kingdom has led the church to greatly value learning and knowledge, but with a tendency to de-value tangible expressions of mission.

The Kingdom exists primarily in and for the heart. This is a more individualistic view: Where Jesus is Lord in the heart there is the Kingdom. The understanding is that the Kingdom is less about bringing change to the world than it is about bringing change to the individual heart. This view of the Kingdom does not look very much to the future; it is concerned with the present state of an individual's heart and relationship with God. It is beyond argument or discussion that the Lord is passionately concerned with the state of our inner selves. After all, the largest collection of His teaching in all of the New Testament, the Sermon on the Mount, is largely focused upon our hearts. However, when the gospel of the Kingdom is understood primarily in this way, the result is often a small gospel that neither expects nor looks for transformation beyond the scope of one's own life.

The Kingdom of God is His transforming presence and power at work in the world. When the Kingdom breaks through, there is justice and peace. Possibilities change. God is the author and the source of His Kingdom, but we have the privilege and responsibility to serve as His representatives. As we follow Jesus as He continues to move forward, we experience the Kingdom's activation both in and through us. The Kingdom is not only given to us, it is also something to be done. The Kingdom of God is not just a set of beliefs; the Kingdom is to be lived out. If the Kingdom is truly in the heart, then the heart changes. A changed heart leads to changed actions empowered by the Holy Spirit, and this brings transformation to society.

WHAT DID JESUS MEAN BY THE KINGDOM OF GOD?

If the Kingdom of God is so foundational to both the teaching and activity of the New Testament, then we must understand what Jesus meant by the Kingdom of God, how it operates, and what its implications are. The message of the Kingdom is not a vague or otherworldly hope. It is powerful and tangible, a life challenging message. So, what did Jesus mean by the "Kingdom of God"?

First of all, the gospel of the Kingdom is a message of fulfillment. In Genesis 12, God promised Abraham that He would bless him, that He would bless his descendants, and through those descendants all peoples of the earth would receive His blessing. God's blessing is His *shalom* – fullness, health, peace. God's covenantal promise to Abraham began its fulfillment with the inauguration of the Kingdom.

Secondly, the gospel of the Kingdom is a message of restoration. The Kingdom of God brings His restoration; it is life as He intended it to be. This is the thrust of all of salvation history: God bringing his whole creation back to what His design had always been. This is why Paul wrote to the Corinthians, *"If anyone is in Christ, he is a new creation; the old has gone, the new has come!"* (2 Cor. 5:17). In the book of Revelation, Jesus declares, *"Behold, I am making all things new"* (Rev. 21:5 ESV). Jesus came announcing that God's gift – His wholeness, His salvation and His reign – has now arrived. God's restoration was manifested through Jesus' preaching and actions.

Thirdly, the word that Jesus used to describe God's breaking in – His Kingdom – was *basileia,* which literally means the royal power, dominion and rule of a king. It is the right or authority to rule. The Kingdom is God's government, which will continue to increase through history (Isa. 9:7); the Kingdom is God's new society. In his book, *The Divine Conspiracy,* Dallas Willard has pointed out that every one of us has a "kingdom" – a realm that is our own; it is where our choices determine what happens. This is because from the beginning God created us to have dominion; the desire to rule is the image of God within us.[3] His Spirit has planted in us a desire and awareness that our lives are to have significance in His creation. Jesus' invitation to enter into the activity of God's Kingdom connects us with our deepest core desire and purpose. He invites us to join Him in His redemptive and creative activity, which is encompassed in His Kingdom. As we say yes, we enter into the activity of His ever-advancing and ever-increasing Kingdom. In Matthew 25, in His parable of the talents, Jesus shows us that as we move into the rhythm of God's Kingdom, we not only share in what He is doing, we also experience His good pleasure.

When Jesus came announcing and demonstrating the gospel of the Kingdom, He was declaring a whole new reality. When Jesus said, "The Kingdom is here, is at hand, is in your midst," He was announcing that the power and reality of the Age to Come – heaven – had now penetrated this present age. Jesus brought the activity of heaven to earth. When a blind eye suddenly opens, that is the demonstration of the reality of heaven penetrating earth because there is no blindness in heaven. G. E. Ladd referred to this breaking in of heaven as "the presence of the future." This helpful term reflects the reality that Jesus was proclaiming the inauguration

---

3 Dallas Willard, *The Divine Conspiracy* (New York: HarperCollins, 1998), 21.

of a Kingdom that is both here and coming at the same time. Jesus brought with Him the Kingdom of God, but not in its final and fullest expression. Because the Kingdom is now here ("at hand"), the rule of God is beginning to break in with healing and justice.

Isaiah 65 and Revelation 21 both describe a day when the New Jerusalem will come down and there will be a new heaven and a new earth — the Kingdom of God fully realized. This is the promise: under the sovereign rule of God, all decay and death will be gone; a whole new creation will be born.

> *Look! I am creating new heavens and a new earth,*
> *and no one will even think about the old ones anymore.*
> *Be glad; rejoice forever in my creation!*
> *And look! I will create Jerusalem as a place of happiness.*
> (Isa. 65:17–18 NLT)

> *Look, God's home is now among his people! He will live with them, and they will be his people. God himself will be with them. He will wipe every tear from their eyes, and there will be no more death or sorrow or crying or pain. All these things are gone forever." And the one sitting on the throne said, "Look, I am making everything new!"*
> (Rev. 21:3–5 NLT)

The Gospel of the Kingdom is the declaration that God is not abandoning His creation; neither is it that He is one day going to take us away, like a great escape, from this irredeemable world and off to heaven. Instead, the message of the Kingdom of God is that there is a glorious future of restoration and fulfillment coming to all of creation. Jesus invites us to participate in the first fruits of its expression through engaging in His work – the signs of the Kingdom. God's great act of new creation was the resurrection of His Son. The resurrection not only bridges the old order and the age to come, it is the prototype of what life in the new creation will be. Jesus' announcement of the Kingdom of God was not centered on believers one day going to heaven; it was a declaration that something new was happening right here on earth. The Kingdom had come and everything was now beginning to change, to move toward the final restoration and resurrection of all things.

In his letter to the Romans Paul wrote:

For all creation is waiting eagerly for that future day when God will reveal who his children really are. Against its will, all creation was subjected to God's curse. But with eager hope, the creation looks forward to the day when it will join God's children in glorious freedom from death and decay. For we know that all creation has been groaning as in the pains of childbirth right up to the present time (Rom. 8:19–22 NLT).

Creation is not groaning because life on earth is coming to an end; clearly, Paul presents a creation in anticipation of the new heaven and earth. Our true identity (Rom. 8:19) is revealed as we demonstrate the signs of this new order, the Kingdom of God. As N.T. Wright has noted "[God] wanted thereby to rescue humans in order that humans might be his rescuing stewards over creation"[4]. Whenever we actively engage in the activity of the Kingdom, we are bringing rescue in the present and moving toward its final fulfillment.

This is why no Kingdom activity is wasted, even when we cannot see any fruit in the present. Paul wrote in 1 Corinthians 15:58, "*Therefore, my dear brothers, stand firm. Let nothing move you. Always give yourselves fully to the work of the Lord, because you know that your labor in the Lord is not in vain.*" Because the good news of the Kingdom is that the earth will be rescued and restored as a new heaven comes down, rather than be destroyed, we can be confident that, through our engagement in the Kingdom

---

4 N.T. Wright, *Surprised By Hope* (New York: HarperCollins, 2008), 202.

activities of healing, rescue, justice, etcetera, we are building for an incorruptible, eternal future. What we do *will* last.

Jesus' announcement of the coming of the Kingdom is an open invitation to everyone and anyone. There is an excitement and urgency in Jesus' message. Jesus is announcing the immediacy of God's great incursion. In Mark, the most active of the four Gospels, with His first words, Jesus makes the joyful announcement, "Here comes the Kingdom!" He is saying that the Kingdom is breaking in, that everything has been prepared for this moment and that God's rule is now available to everyone. I am always struck by the sense of immediacy in these words of Jesus, like breaking news on the radio. And this announcement comes with a call to action. In light of this new reality, Jesus challenges all who hear to evaluate their plans, to change their minds and to now build their lives upon this remarkable announcement.

•   •   •

For Jesus, the declaration and demonstration of the Kingdom were inseparable. The Kingdom comes with signs. That's why He said, *"If you have trouble believing My message, look at the miracles, because they will point to Me and the truth of what I am saying"* (John 10:37–38 paraphrase). This reality of the Kingdom presents everyone with a choice: Will we hold on to our own kingdom, maintaining control of our lives through our own independent decisions; or will we respond to His invitation to enter into God's activity by embracing His priorities and plans? Will we step out from what we know, where we feel comfortable and confident, in order to follow Jesus into the very tangible activity in which He is engaged?

Jesus came to tell us about the life for which we were really created; He called this life, "The Kingdom of God." When we say yes to this invitation we are entering into ultimate and eternal significance. When we embrace His active rule (Kingdom) in our lives, we enter into the "Greater Story" of God, becoming not only participants but also co-workers with Him.

That is why Jesus said, *"I am in the Father and He is in Me"* (John 14:10 GWT). What Jesus did, He did with the Father. In fact, He only did what He saw the Father doing and only said what He heard the Father saying. The Kingdom invitation is an invitation into this shared life with the Person and activity of the eternal Creator God. As we say yes to God's rule and reign in our lives, not only do we participate in the practice of Kingdom activities (like healing, deliverance, justice and mercy), we experience the intimacy of being part of His life and His being a part of ours.

3

THE KINGDOM HAS A KING

Who is he, this King of glory? The LORD Almighty – he is the King of glory. PSALM 24:10

The first truth about the Kingdom is that there is a King. While this may seem obvious, it has significant implications. What we believe about the King will determine the way we live our lives. And conversely, the way we live our lives reveals what we really believe about the King. Jesus once said to Philip, *"Haven't you figured it out yet? If you have seen me you have seen the Father"* (John 14:8 paraphrase). Jesus perfectly revealed the Father in His words and deeds. In his magnificent Christological hymn to the Colossians, the Apostle Paul wrote:

> *Christ is the visible image of the invisible God. He existed before anything was created and is supreme over all creation, for through him God created everything in the heavenly realms and on earth ... For God was pleased to have all his fullness dwell in him* (Col 1:15–16, 19 ESV).

Likewise, the writer to the Hebrews wrote of Christ: *"He is the radiance of the glory of God and the exact imprint of his nature, and he upholds the universe by the word of his power"* (Heb 1:3 ESV). Jesus came not only to lead us to the kingly Father; Jesus came Himself as the full manifestation of the King. As Bill Johnson has said, "Jesus Christ is perfect theology." If we want to understand who God really is and how His Kingdom really works, we simply need to observe Jesus as revealed in the Gospels. What does Jesus teach us about the King?

THE SEEKING KING

In the Old Testament God sent prophets to Israel, calling them to return to Him. In a very real way, God was challenging them to take the initiative, to take the first step to come back to Him. Now Jesus presents a whole new view of the King. No longer does He stand back and wait for them to come; Jesus is the seeking King who is seeking out the sinner. When He was criticized by the religious leaders for being with sinners (Matt. 9), Jesus clearly expressed that His mission was specifically to minister to them. When the church imitates her Master, she gives herself to the outcasts, the "sinners," those who are aware of their need.

In the Gospels we see Jesus continuously moving forward, penetrating the culture around Him. He goes to where the people are. When the religious leaders of the day challenged Jesus about this, He said that *"the Son of Man came to seek and to save what was lost"* (Luke 19:10). We continuously see Jesus moving forward, looking for those that others do not see – the outcasts, the forgotten. In Luke 15, Jesus presents us with three stories about the seeking King: the lost sheep, the lost coin and the prodigal son. The good news is that God has taken the initiative to seek and to save.

This challenges us as individuals to reflect this seeking King. Are we a people who instinctively go out, seeking those who need good news and a living hope? Or do we embrace an Old Testament model, with our church sign announcing Sunday morning service times and leaving it up to the lost and broken to take the first step?

The early church understood what it meant to follow Jesus; it meant going where He goes, being where He is. And Jesus was always out among the people. It is interesting to note that of the twenty-two miracles recorded in the book of Acts, twenty-one of them happened in the marketplace. The early church was simply doing what they had consistently seen Jesus do – running into the darkness of people's lives, not only available but proactively going to people. Wherever Jesus went, the crowds understood that He was there for them, that He was actively engaged. At the end of Mark 6 we read:

> *They ran throughout the whole area, carrying sick people on mats to wherever they heard he was. Wherever he went – in villages, cities, or the countryside – they brought the sick out to the marketplaces. They begged him to let the sick touch at least the fringe of his robe, and all who touched him were healed* (Mark 6:55–56 NLT).

During a two-day training event for about one hundred fifty young adults and teenagers in Nicaragua, among other topics, I taught them about the Kingdom of God, God's passion for justice, and gave them keys for releasing healing. During the second day I surprised them by telling them that it was time to go out into the streets and put what they had learned into practice. I saw a lot of shocked and frightened faces, which was no surprise because they had already told me that they had never done such a thing in their city of one hundred fifty thousand people. I put them in teams of three and told them to ask everyone they see if they could pray for them. They were told to return in just thirty minutes. A very quiet, and frankly, rather unhappy group of people left the church with more than just a little reluctance. As requested, they returned thirty minutes later – but this was a very different group. They were loud and animated, full of energy and excitement. I heard them exchanging stories with one another before I could even invite them to share testimonies. In just half an hour over thirty people were healed out on the street and ten had given their lives to Christ.

As exciting as this is, I believe that this is normal Christianity. This is the Christianity that caused the early church to grow so explosively. We follow the steps of the seeking King when we take the Kingdom to people, especially outside the walls of the church. That is when we see a release of the power and purposes of God. This is what we were made for.

THE INVITING KING

Jesus explained how the Kingdom of God works by telling the story of a great banquet (Matt. 22; Luke 14). A wonderful dinner was prepared and then the King sent out his servants to invite whomever they could find to come. He said go to the main roads and to the out-of-the-way places and invite them all to come. This is such a clear picture of Jesus in the gospels, for surely He was the inviting King. In page after page we see Him reaching out to people and telling them, "You come too. Of course you're included." I do not think there was ever anyone who lived as inclusive a life as Jesus. He walked through life with his arms open wider than anyone else. The invitation was for everyone – prostitutes, tax gatherers, Samaritans and Canaanites, the poor, the sick, the outcasts – no one was excluded. What we believe about the King will determine the way we live our lives both individually and communally. Psalm 68:6 tells us that the King sets the lonely in families. In Psalm 84 we are told that in the King's house there was always a place for the sparrows and the swallows – the poor and the disenfranchised.

When we begin to see the inviting, inclusive Jesus and to follow in his footsteps we will see a revolution in the western church because inclusion touches the great need for security, for belonging. And when we move in the steps of the inviting King we are moving in the rhythm of His Kingdom. I have watched the power of inclusion firsthand, both in the western world and among the poorest of the poor in developing nations. I watched a woman's entire countenance change as she learned that she was not excluded because of her poverty and past mistakes. She was in a refugee camp in Haiti and thought that she was invisible; instead, she was welcomed into a community of believers. Inclusion sees the invisible. Inclusion is the activation of compassion.

THE SERVANT KING

In Mark 10:45 Jesus established a new structure of power and influence. In the Kingdom, up becomes down. He said, *"The Son of Man did not come to be served, but to serve, and to give his life as a ransom for many."* Jesus introduced the servant King. We see Him serving the weakest and the overlooked, whether they be children, an adulterous woman, or an outcast leper. The servant King came for many, not just His own followers. If we are going to follow the servant King, we must move beyond the familiar, the well known; we must move radically outside of our comfort zone because He came to give His life as a ransom for many and not just those close at hand.

Demonstrating the heart of the servant King always brings a powerful response from people. Jesus *came* for people. One of the clearest ways this is demonstrated is through serving them. In the 1980's I met Steve Sjogren. It was a meeting that would impact the way I have ministered since then. Steve had discovered the power of the servant King. Following his example in every church and ministry that I have led, I have sought to lead the church outside the walls, to take the Kingdom to the community. When we understand Jesus as the servant King, our eyes begin to see our neighborhoods and cities in entirely new ways. The ways to serve those around us are almost limitless. Whether it is grocery hampers to the hungry, giving out cold soft drinks on a hot day, cleaning a yard, or setting up a community picnic in the park, there are so many ways to reflect Jesus' servant heart. People are always surprised and ask why we are doing these things. When we tell them that they are just a small way to remind them today how much God loves them and cares about them, the response is always positive. This is because, I am convinced, that everyone, everywhere is made for the gospel of the Kingdom, whether they know it or not. It is in everyone's DNA; it is the Creator's stamp upon our lives.

Whenever we step out to serve, there is favor and blessing. This is because we are moving in the rhythm of the King, the one who came *"to serve and to give his life as a ransom for many"* (Mark 10:45 ESV). I live in the least churched major city in all of North America; however, whenever I go out with friends to serve with acts of kindness into my city, we always have significant encounters. Taking bag lunches to a housing project to give to parents for their children at school the next day, we are sometimes led to twenty or thirty significant encounters. I have come away from such times with my shirt wet with people's tears, after praying for them and listening to the pain and brokenness in their lives. During these times we see people healed and give their lives to Jesus. I do not know how many times I have had someone say, "This is the first time anyone has ever prayed for me." I have watched men and women in wealthy neighborhoods share their pain and fear simply because someone expressed the tangible love of Jesus through something as simple as raking their leaves or shoveling the walk. I believe there is something supernatural in this. Again, when we move in the rhythm of the King doors open, favor comes.

THE FATHER KING

Jesus came to introduce us to the Father. This was a radical declaration in first century Israel. And now, in the twenty-first century, a time of unprecedented family breakdown, this again has become a radical and very necessary message. There is an inseparable link between the Kingdom of God and fatherhood. Matthew 13:43 says that the righteous will enter the Kingdom of their Father. Luke 12:32 tells us that the Father will bestow the gift of the Kingdom on all who follow Jesus. Famously in the Lord's Prayer, Jesus taught His disciples to pray, "Our Father who art in heaven, Thy Kingdom come." These sayings reveal an important fact about the Father and His Kingdom. His fatherhood is a blessing and a special relationship that is enjoyed by those who enter His Kingdom. God loves everybody but He is only obliged to His children. In John's Gospel where the writer presents the Kingdom in terms of eternal life and abundant life, we see repeatedly the link between fatherhood and abundant life. Jesus came to present the God of the universe as our Father. It is the Father who bestows blessings on His children. It is sons and daughters who receive the Kingdom with all its richness and blessing. We are made for the Father and the gospel of the Kingdom is intertwined with the message of the father-heart of God.

THE RESCUING KING

"For the Son of Man came to find and restore the lost" (Luke 19:10 MSG).

As I have already stated, no one lived as inviting and inclusive a life as Jesus. The gospel was and is for everyone. In Jericho one day, Jesus reached out to what was probably the most unpopular man in the town, a tax-gatherer named Zachaeus. Oh, the crowd was very happy that Jesus' arms were wide enough to include them, but when His reach extended to someone so universally rejected, they began to mutter. They were excited to be included, but they did not understand His reason for living inclusively.

Jesus came on a rescue mission. Recognizing this helps us to understand the greater significance of His words and actions. The Father had sent Jesus on assignment and He never lost sight of this. From the beginning of His ministry Jesus went throughout the northern region of Galilee teaching and preaching about the Kingdom of God, and healing every disease and sickness among the people. A few years after Jesus' resurrection, Peter described His rescue mission like this:

> *You know about Jesus from Nazareth, that God gave him the Holy Spirit and power. You know how Jesus went everywhere doing good and healing those who were ruled by the devil, because God was with him* (Acts 10:38 NCV).

John, in his first letter, put it like this *"The reason that the Son of God appeared was to destroy what the devil does"* (1 John 3:8 GWT).

Jesus came to rescue people from the influence and works of Satan in their lives – sickness, pain, oppression, and despair. Every healing, every encounter is about Jesus' taking back from the enemy what belongs to God. Every account of Jesus' authority has one common element: people are set free from whatever binds them. When a man that was cleansed of his leprosy or a blind man began to see, the significance went beyond the healing they received; their very lives were rescued. A new future was created for them in just a moment.

It had been a long and exciting gathering in the hills of West Kenya. Many of these rural people walking for over two hours through the steep, hilly country had experienced God's Kingdom as it came in great power. I remember being brought to a woman who was burning up and yet shivering; like so many others in sub-Saharan Africa, she was suffering terribly from malaria. Her friend who had beckoned me looked on anxiously, as I prayed and invited the Kingdom of Heaven to come to this sick woman. Even as I prayed we both felt her temperature drop dramatically. As I continued to pray she opened her eyes and said, "All of the pain in my body is leaving." A couple of minutes later she stood up saying that she had no more malaria symptoms whatsoever.

A short while later, it was time for the Impact team to get in the vans and begin the hour-long journey back to town. It had been a particularly exciting and very full day of ministry, and it was now becoming quite late in the evening. As we were walking toward the vans, a man took hold of my arm and asked me to please come and pray for his wife. In all honesty, I was very tired and the meeting was breaking up, so I told the man that I would be back the next day. He looked at me very intently, grasped my arm tighter and said, "No, you must come, now." Jesus told us that the Kingdom of God is forcefully advancing and that forceful men and women take hold of it (Matt. 11:12). This man was desperate and he would not be denied. He led me to his thirty-five-year-old wife. Three weeks earlier she had suffered a stroke and was paralyzed down one side of her body. As I put my hand on her head and began to pray, suddenly she fell to the ground and lay completely still. Some of the people standing nearby said that she had died. But I assured them that this was God's Spirit working in her body right now. A couple of minutes later, the woman opened her eyes and looked around. At first, she sat, and then, stood up. She moved her arms and legs freely; all of the paralysis was gone.

At one level we can say that she had been healed, but I see healing in a larger paradigm. Once again, this was the work of the Rescuing King. What had been stolen from this young wife and mother had now been recovered by the compassionate power of Jesus. In a moment the possibilities and direction of her future had changed forever.

When we pray for the sick, we need to do so with a deep awareness of the rescue mission. As I write this, I think back to the blind who received their sight in India. More than a healing, these encounters changed the very way that these people could now interact in their communities. Recently, as I walked through the village in South India, asking if anyone needed healing, a woman from nearby was brought to me who was totally blind. When I began to pray for her she explained that she could see light. As I continued to pray she could see shadows, then shapes and color. That night as I sat up on a small stage with some of our Impact

Nations team, this woman began to wave and smile at me from the crowd. I was excited that she could see, but what really thrilled me was the knowledge that this woman could now live her life as a wife, mother and member of her community in an entirely new way. Likewise, when a little boy with a withered hand was healed a few months ago in Uganda, the possibilities for his future changed in instant. A single encounter with the Kingdom of God can change a life forever.

What we believe about the King and His Kingdom will determine the way we live our lives. Pastors and leaders in the West spend so much time struggling with the issues of the relevance of the church to society and a sense of purpose for its members. Despite our best plans and efforts, the Western church has been in numerical decline for more than thirty years. When the church, both in the West and in the developing world, embraces what it is to truly follow and reflect the seeking, inviting, serving, rescuing King who is holy and loves justice, *then* we will become the counter-cultural change agents (salt and light) that the early church was, and that Jesus has always intended it to be. *Then* we, like Jesus the King, will become immediately relevant to a world that is looking for something beyond merely more words. And our church members will come alive as they connect to the great cause of the Gospel of the Kingdom.

4

MOVING IN THE RHYTHM OF THE KINGDOM

Heal the sick, and tell them, "The Kingdom of God is near you now." LUKE 10:9 NLT

One of the questions that I am repeatedly asked is, "Why don't we see miracles in the West like we do in the developing world?" This is a question that people have wrestled with for a long time, especially with the rise of missionary work among the Pentecostal and Charismatic streams of the evangelical church over the past hundred years. I certainly do not suggest that I know the complete answer to this difficult question.

Perhaps in the developing world there is a more simple and accepting faith that creates an atmosphere for healing. As well, in poor communities where no medical treatment is available, when people become seriously ill or injured, unlike for most of us in the West, God is the only hope. I have certainly found over the years that when I present the gospel in villages and urban slums overseas, and tell them that Jesus will heal them, there is generally no resistance to the message. Sadly, I cannot say the same thing, even in the church, when I share in a similar fashion in North America, Europe or Australia.

I think there is another issue to consider. The Bible clearly teaches about the sovereignty of God; that God is in control is one of the great foundational tenets of the Christian faith. However, we must be careful that this does not lead us into a place of passivity. One of the miracles of the gospel is that the sovereign, Creator God chooses to work with and through us. This goes all the way back to Genesis 12 where the Lord spoke to Abraham (our spiritual father), promising that He would bless Abraham and his descendants, and through his descendants would bless all people groups of the earth. God has always come to a people, moved through a people and moved from them to other people groups.

As we've already seen, Jesus was not passive but active, moving forward as the seeking, inviting, serving King. Jesus brought the Kingdom to us and whenever He ministered, the Kingdom was activated. In the same way that the Father sent Him, so Jesus has sent us into our world to release the activity of God's Kingdom.

Matthew primarily identifies God's Kingdom as the Kingdom of heaven, in contrast to Mark and Luke's the Kingdom of God. This was partly because the Kingdom of heaven was a more acceptable term to his Jewish audience. However, there is something else very significant. Whereas most Bible translations read "the Kingdom of heaven," the original Greek language should be translated as the Kingdom of *the* heavens, which reflects the New Testament understanding that God's presence is all around us. He is both transcendent and immanent. We can never know when He and His Kingdom will suddenly break in. The heavens speaks both of his grandeur and of his nearness.

Jesus said, *"the Kingdom of God is forcefully advancing and forceful men (and women) take hold of it"* (Matt. 11:12 NIV). If we are going to see the Kingdom of God manifested in our world, there is a forcefulness, almost an aggressiveness that is required. This is not an aggressiveness of style or personality but of purpose. It is an aggressiveness that refuses to take no for an answer when we are seeking breakthrough. It is a forcefulness that prays bold prayers, expecting great things to happen. In the Gospels, Jesus always seemed to look for this kind of forcefulness. When Jesus encountered the Canaanite woman whose daughter needed to be healed, He seemed to be putting her off, to be saying no. But I think Jesus was merely stirring up the forcible desperation that was in her. And so I imagine he was smiling as He said, "Lady, you really have a lot of faith!" When blind Bartimaeus was told to keep quiet, he shouted out for Jesus all the louder. I hear something even beyond desperation in his cry – it is almost demand. Others are offended by this, but not Jesus. Result? Bartimaeus received the very thing he asked for. Something else stands out in this story: after calling Bartimaeus to himself, Jesus asked him, "What do you want?" The need was obvious to anyone who looked into this man's blind eyes, so why did Jesus ask this? There is something that provokes heaven when we clearly declare our greatest desire. This is a question that goes beyond healing. God asks us today, "What do you really want?" Do we want to see His Kingdom come? Do we want to see His name famous on the earth? Do we long to see His justice, His intervention, His rescue for the poor and the oppressed?

THE RESPONSIBILITY OF REVELATION

The watershed of Matthew's Gospel is chapter 16, versus 15–19. The narrative builds slowly and steadily to this point; and from this moment on there is a great acceleration. Jesus overhears his twelve friends talking about the various rumors circulating about his identity. Jesus then asks them "Who do you say I am?" We can almost feel all of heaven holding its breath. Until now no one had ever spoken the answer to this question. Of course, this is the question that every one of us will one day have to answer before the throne of God. In verse 16 Peter answers Jesus – "You are the Christ, the Son of the living God." I imagine a great cheer going up in heaven. Jesus then says three very interesting things: first He tells Peter "You didn't figure that out on your own Peter.

That was revelation given to you." Then Jesus tells Peter that this revelation of His true identity is so powerful that it will serve as the foundation for something new: the church.

Finally, in verse 19 Jesus says the most surprising thing of all. After being identified as the Christ, we could reasonably expect Jesus to respond by saying "That's right Peter. I am the Christ and I have so much authority that whenever I bind or loose that's what happens." But that is *not* what Jesus said. He said, "Whatever you bind or release on earth that's what gets bound or released in heaven. The preposition suggests both 'in' and 'from' heaven. Jesus was saying something absolutely amazing. "Peter you're right, this came to you as revelation from heaven. But with this revelation comes a whole new responsibility. From now on, whatever *you* release on earth, that is what gets released in and from heaven."

I find this to be one of the most radical and empowering passages in the New Testament. When I first saw this it changed the way I saw ministry; it changed the possibilities. Although I have been praying for the sick since 1977, when I saw the truth of this passage I began to see a huge increase in healing. I also saw a vast increase in the number of people who gave their lives to Christ.

Life seems to be made up of episodes that permanently mark us. I had one of these in Mexico a few years ago. We had taken the team for twelve days of ministry. On the first evening at a rather large evangelistic gathering, one of our team, a relatively young Christian, received a word of knowledge that God wanted to heal someone from muteness. A boy of about ten or eleven was brought forward and the team member prayed for him. Instantly the boy could speak perfect and fluent Spanish. He was obviously well known in the community because the entire meeting erupted; I may always remember the sight of his mother sobbing with joy as her son spoke. The next night in another town after giving an invitation to the crowd to give their lives to Christ, a large group came forward. While I was praying a blessing over them I became aware of a bit of a commotion over to one side. I looked over the heads of the people and saw a girl crying and being embraced by her mother, father and grandmother. They told the gathering that this thirteen-year-old girl had been completely deaf for ten years ever since being stricken with meningitis. The crowd erupted with clapping and shouts. Immediately I felt a sadness that I could not understand. So while the people continued to celebrate, I quietly walked over to the side of the platform and asked the Lord, "I don't understand. Why do I suddenly feel so sad?" It seemed so incongruous with what was going on. I will never forget what the Lord said to me: "Do you remember that boy last night who could not speak and now he can?" "Yes Papa, of course I do." "And you see that girl who has been deaf for ten years and now she can hear?" "Yes, of course." "What happened last night and tonight could have happened years ago, but there was no one willing to release it."

Those words marked me, and by God's grace I hope they will mark me forever. How much of the Kingdom of the heavens would we see if the only we would step out and release the works of God? How many lives, how many families, how many villages and towns would be impacted and transformed by the power and reality of God's Kingdom, if we the church would abandon ourselves to a forceful, desperate faith that anticipates and is sensitive to heaven breaking in at any moment, in any place? Romans 14:17 tells us that the Kingdom of God is in the power and reality of the Holy Spirit. Ephesians 1:14 tells us the Holy Spirit has been given to us as a down payment of our ultimate inheritance. The Kingdom of God is given to us. We were made for the transforming, radical, everything-changing Kingdom of God.

THE KINGDOM COMES WITH GRACE

In Mark's Gospel, which is most likely the earliest Gospel account, we are presented in the first chapter with a small but very interesting verse. *"The Kingdom of God is at hand. Repent and believe in the gospel"* (Mark 1:15 ESV). Jesus came bringing the Kingdom. He brought it with both his words and the actions of His life. The term "at hand" does not mean is coming soon so much as it means that the Kingdom is breaking in right now. The very declaration of the Kingdom brings its reality. It calls for a response. As Frederick Bruner points out in his commentary on Matthew, Jesus' declaration that the Kingdom is at hand was much like when Paul Revere rode through the streets of Boston warning the citizens, "The British are coming! The British are coming!" There is an immediacy, almost an urgency in these, the first recorded words of Jesus in Mark's Gospel. Jesus is calling for an immediate response to the reality of God's Kingdom breaking in.

These words of Jesus strike me as being words of grace. For the gospel of the Kingdom is full of grace. Note the order: Jesus declares the Kingdom is at hand, therefore repent and believe. The Kingdom *is coming*; it is yours, it is tangible, it is unshakable. The Kingdom is always moving forward. The only thing that is in question is our response to its coming. Notice Jesus did not say if you will repent and believe, then you will see the Kingdom; that would have been conditional grace. The declaration of the Kingdom is about unconditional grace. I have sat in meetings where a well-intentioned preacher has told the crowd, "If you will give your life to Jesus tonight, He will heal you." This is not the gospel that Jesus preached and demonstrated, but it is the gospel that all too often believers present to the world.

How often do we tell friends and associates who are going through difficulties or are sick, "Why don't you come to my church on Sunday. Someone will pray for you there." When the lepers, when the blind, when the paralyzed and deaf came to Jesus, how often did He say "I will heal you but first I want you to pray the sinner's prayer and then I want you to promise to go to the synagogue every Sabbath"? Without exception, we see Jesus unconditionally releasing the power and reality of the Kingdom in healing and restoration to all those in need. This is the "empowered compassion" that Jesus walked in and that He calls us to walk in. Notice that not everyone who received healing (which is a tangible sign of the Kingdom's presence) turned to Jesus in repentance. When He prayed for ten lepers who were healed as they went away from him and nine of them did not come back, do we think that Jesus was surprised by that? Of course not. He knows the hearts of every man and woman, and yet it His joy to release the Kingdom to all who will receive it.

A fundamental principle is this: the tangible presence of the Kingdom initiates repentance in the hearts of people, not vice versa. If we want to see people open their hearts to Christ, then we must be willing to demonstrate the Kingdom. That is why when Jesus sent out the seventy-two on their first ministry trip, He told them to first heal the sick and then say to them *"the Kingdom of God has come to you"* (Luke 10:9). The foundation of the gospel is to demonstrate the love of God. People do not remember what they hear about God's love. Christian sociologists will tell us that within ninety minutes of hearing the four spiritual laws, the majority of people cannot remember even one of them. However people always remember what they *experience* of the love of God, whether through healing, serving, or compassion. It is time for us to trust the power of the demonstration of God's Kingdom to impact hearts and lives.

Jesus once told the story about a farmer who went out to scatter seed. As he threw the seed out, some of it landed on the road, some of it landed on very shallow rocky soil, some of it landed among the weeds and the thorns, and only some of it landed on the good soil where it produced a great harvest. Most of us have heard a number of sermons about this parable which reflects four different responses to hearing the gospel. This is clearly what Jesus' parable is about; however I see another over-arching principle displayed in this story. When I was a boy growing up in the city, every summer I went to visit my cousin's farm. As I got older I was allowed to do some of the various chores that for me as a city boy were an adventure. I knew almost nothing about farming, but I knew that if took my cousin's precious seed and scattered it so carelessly that some landed on the road, the rocks and weeds, that I would be in big trouble. So what is happening in this story? I believe more than anything, the parable of the farmer is about the fiery, extravagant love of God. In His passion for all people, He is like a farmer who cannot help himself – in His passion for people, He has to scatter the seed everywhere. We have historically been so careful with the seed, praying over each one. Sometimes we pray, "Father, show me the one you want me to pray for today." But the Kingdom is about extravagance; the Kingdom is for everyone and we are to be like the farmer who scatters its seed everywhere we go.

THE "ALL BY ITSELF" PRINCIPLE

In Mark 4:28 Jesus says the Kingdom is like a farmer who plants the seed and goes away and *all by itself* it springs up. We need to recognize the "all by itself principle" of the Kingdom. When people experience the tangible signs of the Kingdom, so often their hearts are deeply touched and they turn to Christ. But even if they do not turn to Him, it is God's desire to bless people. Remember, God came for people. Over the past several years, as I have taken teams to a number of nations in the developing world, I have seen many hundreds of Muslims come to Christ. I have seen many Buddhists come to Christ. I have seen thousands upon thousands of Hindus come to Christ. At no time have I ever debated with any of them, comparing religion or writings – frankly I don't know enough about the Koran or the Bhagavad Gita to do that effectively. But I *do* know Mark 1:15. Instead of debating, I have simply asked

"What do you need? What does your child need? What does your mother need?" And when they or their loved one is healed I tell them "That was a gift to you from Jesus. He has another gift. He would like to come and live inside you and be with you from now on. Would you like that gift?" Because they have just received a demonstration of the Kingdom of God and His great love for them, they almost always say "yes." And I do mean almost always. In the last six years I only recall four times when a Muslim having just been healed has politely declined to receive Christ.

Let me illustrate how powerful the "all by itself" principle of Mark 4:28 really is. On my first trip to India in 1998, I learned a lesson about the power of the Gospel. My friend Leslie and I were driving a couple of hours from Delhi so that I could teach at a Bible school. Part way along the journey my friend said that he had to go into a village for a few minutes to do some business and hoped I wouldn't mind waiting for him. This was actually my first time going into a rural Indian village. I was immediately struck by how "locked in time" the village was – I saw no signs of electricity, the small houses were packed along dirt laneways. As I waited for Leslie the villagers began to gather in front of me. No one said anything; in a couple of minutes there were thirty or forty of them simply staring at me – I found it rather disconcerting. At that point all I wanted was for Leslie to come back so that we could get to the Bible school. Then the Lord impressed on me that there was a boy I was to pray for. "What do you want me to pray, Papa?" I got no answer, so feeling rather nervous I walked over to the boy and began to pray for him in English, which of course no one understood. But I believe that small act of obedience released the activity of heaven in that village because as soon as I finished praying my short prayer, Leslie came around the corner. As he walked up to me I asked him to translate: "Jesus Christ, the son of God is here in this place today to heal you. What do you need?" I can assure you that I was almost as surprised as the villagers when those words came out of my mouth.

An older man came forward with his arms crippled – it looked to me that it was severe arthritis – and I said to him "It is Jesus Christ who is the son of God; He is about to heal you right now." I prayed a short prayer and immediately his arms went up over his head and he said, "I'm healed! I'm healed!" (Remember, I had Leslie as my mouth and ears). A woman came forward with pain; I prayed and she was healed – then another and another. As always happens when Jesus is healing, the crowds began to gather. Every prayer was short, every healing was almost immediate. In every case before I prayed, I told them that it was Jesus the Son of God who was healing. I stood there and prayed for one after another for about ninety minutes. Leslie was looking concerned as he realized we would be very late at the Bible school. Finally he insisted that we leave and headed toward the car with the crowd following. As we drove away Leslie was so excited, and frankly so was I. He said to me, "Did you hear what all those villagers kept saying over and over?" I said to Leslie "I don't understand the language how could I know what they were saying? "They kept saying it is Jesus who is healing! It is Jesus who is healing!"

I am sure that you've noticed there is something missing in this story. Because I was pulled away from what was happening so suddenly, I did not present the gospel. Had I known about the suddenness of our departure of course I would've done so, but in fact this never happened. But Mark 1:15 and Mark 4:28 are very powerful. Here is how the story ends: Two months later back in my home in Vancouver, Canada, my phone rang one night. It was a man I knew in India. He told me that two nights previously he had been to that village and he wanted to tell me about two things he had seen there. "First, there were more people healed that day than you could have known. There were children who were dying of dysentery that are completely well. There were deaf ears opened." I thanked him, then he told me the second thing he saw – which was the main reason for calling. "When I came to the village they were gathered together and they were healing the sick, telling them "It is Jesus who is healing you." Because of that, my friend sent a pastor to work with those people and teach them the full gospel of salvation.

Our assignment is to scatter the seed of the Kingdom extravagantly; when we do, the supernatural, irresistible life that is in that seed does its work "all by itself."

THE KINGDOM COMES WITH RISK

The Kingdom of God is advancing and as it goes forward it comes into conflict with the kingdom of darkness and all those political, economic and religious systems under that kingdom's influence. With every healing and salvation God's Kingdom goes forward. Jesus explicitly stated that when demons are cast out, the Kingdom has come (Luke 11:20). The advancing Kingdom of God pushes back the sickness, oppression, despair, injustice and poverty of the enemy's Kingdom. It is real. It is tangible. When we do the works of the Kingdom, we are stepping into conflict.

All advancement means change; and change is always risky. This should not surprise us. It was always risky following Jesus. We read the Gospels from the perspective of already knowing how each story ends. The problem with this is that the characters in the Gospel stories can easily become two-dimensional, like comic book characters. But they were real men and women struggling with the same issues that all men and women deal with. When Jesus said "Follow Me" and people responded, He was leading them into a whole way of life, one that challenged their presuppositions and assumptions.

In the beginning of Mark 11 we read about Jesus sending two of his disciples into the next village to retrieve a colt. Jesus was going to use this donkey colt for His triumphal entry into

Jerusalem, thus fulfilling Zechariah's prophecy of Jesus coming as a humble Messiah King (Zech. 9:9). It is also possible that Jesus was engaging in sociopolitical parody. In the Roman world, a ruler would enter the city on a white war horse. As Jesus reveals himself to Jerusalem as the Messiah, he does so with a twist, contrasting the values and power of the world with those of the upside-down Kingdom of God. Jesus tells them where they will find the colt tied up then instructs them to simply untie it and bring it to Him. If anyone asks, "Hey! What you think you're doing?" they are to simply say that the Master needs it. Imagine at this point that you were one of those two disciples given this assignment. Jesus has just told you to go into the next town to the parking lot in front of a large shopping center. There you'll find a brand new silver Lexus with the keys in the ignition. Start it up and bring it to him. This is a fairly accurate comparison since in first century Judea colts were so valuable that they were often shared by two or even three families. Following Jesus always meant taking risks.

The one episode that is recorded in all four Gospels is the feeding of the five thousand. This great miracle is familiar to all who have read the Bible; beginning with five loaves and two fish over five thousand people are fed and when they have finished eating there are twelve baskets of food left over. But again, let us consider this miracle from the point of view of one of the disciples. Luke's version of this episode seems to make it clear that Jesus prayed over the loaves and fish, then handed them to the disciples to distribute. It was as they distributed the food that the miracle took place. This is an exciting story, pointing clearly to Jesus' care for the physical needs of people and calling us to share in that care. But this too, is a story about the risk of following Jesus.

Imagine you are Andrew holding a little bit of fish and bread in one hand as Jesus directs you to a crowd of perhaps five hundred people and says, "Andrew, go feed them." If I was Andrew walking toward that crowd I know I would feel fear and probably embarrassment, knowing that what I was doing was ridiculous. How could this little bit feed all those people? And so with great reluctance I apologetically hand this bit of food to the first person and start to get out of there as quickly as I can. But after only a couple of steps I look down, perplexed to see that there's still some bread and fish in my hand. Slightly confused, I return and give it to the next person and again begin to retreat. When I see for the third time fish and bread in my hand I start to realize there is something supernatural going on here. We can imagine the joy and sheer fun of tossing food out to person after person, knowing that it will never end until everyone's fed.

But let's go back to the beginning. Andrew had a choice. He could take the risk even though what Jesus had told him to do seemed to make no sense, or he could have said this can't be done and simply put the bit of bread and fish in his pocket. In almost every situation that God presents to us, whether at work or school, at the supermarket or the gas station, we are presented with the same decision. But at this point we need to remember that it was in the act of giving away the little that he had that the food was multiplied. Faced with someone's sickness or infirmity, in fact, faced with a great need of almost any type, we must choose to give away what we have in spite of our feelings of inadequacy – because what we have is multiplied in the giving.

Several years ago I was teaching about this in a class at my church. There was a new believer, Lorraine, who that night prayed "Father, if you will speak to me I will do whatever you say." As a new believer, Lorraine did not understand the significant risk involved in that prayer. A couple of days later she was at a coffee shop and as she left Lorraine sensed the Lord point a particular woman out to her. "Lorraine, that woman is afraid for her marriage. I want you to go tell her she doesn't have to be afraid." Now Lorraine had a dilemma. She kept walking right out of that coffee shop and stood in the parking lot arguing with God that she couldn't possibly walk up to a strange woman and say that to her. Suddenly she remembered the promise she had made a few nights earlier and so with a sense of resignation she said "Okay Lord, I'll do it." As she started to walk back into the coffee shop, feeling nothing but fear, Lorraine began to rehearse in her mind what she would say to this stranger. To her surprise, as she walked up to the woman these words came out of her mouth: "Anne." The woman turned, looked at Lorraine and said "Yes?" "You don't have to be afraid about you and Don. God has his hand on both of you and He's going to work everything out." When we give away the bit of bread and fish that we have, God always multiplies it in the very act of giving.

In Matthew 25 Jesus told the story of three servants who each received large sums of money from their master with the assignment to invest it while he was away. The first two men immediately took what they were given and invested it. Investment is risk-taking. When their master returned he was delighted with the first two servants, not only because they made a good return but because they were willing to take risks on his behalf. Sadly, the third servant was too afraid of making mistakes and so he could not bring himself to take action. He was not only severely rebuked, the master also took back what he had first given him. Those who will advance in Kingdom activity are those who are willing to take risks. Period. This is why we have taken many hundreds of men and women on Journeys of Compassion with Impact Nations to developing countries all over the world. We put them in an environment of daily risk-taking and every day we watch them grow in confidence and authority as they discover that God indeed releases Kingdom activity through them.

A significant key to seeing the church increase its impact in the Western world is to foster an atmosphere that celebrates risk-taking. More than twenty years ago Tom Peters coined the phrase: "Ready, Fire, Aim." There is an immediacy to Kingdom activity

(Mark's Gospel uses the word "immediately" forty-one times). If we're going to celebrate those who are willing to take risks in our church, then we must have a high tolerance for mistakes. Personally I think that mistakes are a healthy sign; they indicate that we are trying to do what we haven't done before. When people are affirmed for stepping out in faith, for trying something that they've never done before, they grow in confidence and security, and the Kingdom advances.

As I have already said, we have a very real enemy with an agenda to reduce and neutralize our faith, vision and dreams for what is possible. He seems to have three main strategies to keep us from taking the risk of stepping into Kingdom activity: the first is fear. When we decide to step out and pray for that person at the supermarket, especially if this is something new for us, we can anticipate a sudden and strong feeling of fear. "What if nothing happens? What if they say no? What if I'm embarrassed?" In this way our enemy stops a lot of Kingdom activity in its tracks. If this doesn't work and we do step out, he usually moves to discouragement. He tries to convince us that what we are doing is ineffective, that the problem is too big, that we are failing. This is why it is so important for us to keep our eyes focused on Jesus, the one who says "Follow me and go where I'm going, do what I'm doing." If neither of these strategies stop us from moving ahead then our enemy uses distraction. We become too busy or there's too many interruptions or it becomes too inconvenient. When we sense this happening we need to make the shift from what is immediately urgent to what is eternally important.

THE "GO" OF THE KINGDOM

Three times in the Gospels Jesus emphatically says "Go." In Matthew 9:13 He says this: *"Go and learn what this means, I desire mercy and not sacrifice."* Jesus was saying this to the religious crowd, telling them that a life of mercy and activated compassion were much more important to God than religious activity. But notice the significant word order – "*Go* and learn." Jesus did not say learn and learn some more and when you have learned enough, then go. He was saying "Go, and you will learn in the going." In many ways I think we have complicated the Gospel, both its message and methodology. I believe that we need to learn, but I also believe that most learning happens as we go out into the harvest field. There's a great tendency in the church for us to hide behind training, telling ourselves that if we just read one or two more books or attend the next conference then we will be ready to go. This is like saying "Ready, Aim… Ready, Aim… Ready, Aim…." To be about the business of the Kingdom, we have to "Fire."

At the end of his story about the Good Samaritan, Jesus says this, *"Go* and do likewise" (Luke 10:37). The Good Samaritan got involved in the pain and distress of the man lying on the side of the road. He cared for him, cleaning his wounds, putting him on his own donkey, carrying him to the nearest inn, and paying for his keep. If we are going to go we must be prepared to *do*. The call of the Kingdom is a call to action. It is a call to compassion that goes beyond feelings. It is a call to learn to see what is all around us – as Mother Theresa said, "to see Jesus in a distressing disguise."

At the end of Matthew's Gospel Jesus addressed his disciples with what is called "The Great Commission" (Matt 28:18–20). Jesus told them: *"Go* and make disciples of all nations." He told the disciples to baptize people and teach them all that they had learned. His final words were these, *"I am with you always to the end of the age."* First Jesus told them to go and then He promised them that He would always be with them in the going. We may feel closer to Jesus as we gather together, and certainly He is in our midst in our gatherings. But *where* He promises to be with us is *out there*, when we *go*. Disciples follow Jesus into the harvest field. They are willing to run into the darkness (John 1:5) in order to bring tangible demonstrations of the Kingdom of God to people. We go because Jesus came for people and we are called to be His co-laborers. In Matthew 10:7–8, Jesus said, *"As you go"* and then listed the Kingdom activities of healing and setting the oppressed free. *As you go* is the key that releases everything else. In John's prologue he said this about Jesus, "and the word became flesh and dwelt among us." E. Stanley Jones translated that verse as "the ideal became real." Eugene Peterson in The Message said it this way, "God moved into the neighborhood."

This is one of the great watersheds for the church. Will we activate our faith? In spite of fear, discomfort and insecurity will we move beyond the walls of theory and concept and step into the world of Jesus, following Him among the sick, the poor, the oppressed and the hopeless? Either we will, and therefore become the fruitful people that will bring real glory to him and the Father (John 15:8), or we won't and settle for ideas and putting things off until next month.

Jesus seems to delight in sending the inexperienced to advance his Kingdom. In Luke 10 we read about the seventy-two returning from their first field trip. They are full of the joy and excitement that always happens when God uses us. As they returned Luke records Jesus response: *"At that time Jesus, full of joy through the Holy Spirit, said, 'I praise you Father, Lord of heaven and earth, because you have hidden these things from the wise and learned and have revealed them to little children. Yes Father, for this was your good pleasure'"* (Luke 10:21). On every Journey of Compassion we have brand-new believers and sometimes those who are still just seeking, as part of our team. One of my great delights is watching as again and again God uses them, as they step out in simple faith, to heal the sick. Several days into a recent Journey of Compassion I looked at the young woman on our team who had clearly declared herself as not yet a Christian during the team orientation. Now just a few days later as I looked across the field I saw her laying hands on the sick and them being healed. She chose to follow Jesus, discovering that his Kingdom is real and that God uses her to advance it. From the beginning of her new life, she *experienced* the reality of the Kingdom – the Word became flesh; the ideal became real.

Once, I took a team into a maximum-security prison in the Philippines. There had been a misunderstanding and the inmates thought that we were conducting a medical clinic; however, the medical clinic was going on in another community. We invited them to gather as we sang and presented the gospel; though disappointed about the clinic, they decided to attend the gathering. One of our team shared a powerful testimony of how God had brought him from great despair as an inmate in a different prison to a place where God was using him powerfully to rescue lives. He finished his testimony with an invitation for these men to invite Christ into their lives, which many of them did. I then invited those who were sick to come forward to receive healing prayer; many came. Although they were expecting that I and our team would pray for them, I sensed God had something else in mind. I asked those who had received Christ a few minutes earlier to come forward and stand in front of the inmates who needed healing. I then explained to these two-minute-old Christians that they now had the same spirit of Christ in them as me or any of the team. I gave them a brief and simple outline of how to pray for their fellow inmates and invited them to do so. As simply as that, each of them began to pray for a sick or injured inmate. *Every one* was healed. I then explained that the Kingdom of God had come into their midst, and when the Kingdom comes, what was impossible before it is now possible. I told him there was now a whole new reality in this prison. No longer do they have to wait and wait, hoping that someone will come and provide medical care. From now on whenever any of them are sick or injured they simply need to pray as I just showed them and God will move. A great cheer arose; I think the guards were cheering the loudest of all.

Perhaps this simplicity of faith, this willingness of brand-new believers to step out is what Jesus had in mind when he said that the Kingdom belongs to those who approach it like little children.

THE MULTIPLICATION OF THE KINGDOM

When Jesus came, he brought the Kingdom of God with Him. Through His preaching, healing, and deliverance, He both declared a new reality and demonstrated its veracity. The Kingdom of God had come to earth and it had a name and a face: Jesus. The Kingdom of God now had one representative. After about eighteen months of training His disciples by continually and actively exposing them to the works of the Kingdom, Jesus sent them out on their first field trip. He told them to go out and do what they had seen him do over the past year and a half. When he sent them, he gave them power and authority to do the works of the Kingdom. He specifically instructed them to both proclaim the Kingdom of God and to heal the sick. Once again, we are back to the issue of risk taking; and certainly the Twelve must have felt a keen sense of risk as for the first time they went out on their own. Some days later they returned having made a wonderful and powerful discovery: They too could release the Kingdom of God in their midst. Now the Kingdom of God had thirteen representatives.

Sometime later Jesus gathered seventy-two other disciples and sent them out with similar instructions, encouraging them that there was a plentiful harvest waiting for them. He told them to look for receptive people, because surely there is a receptiveness all around them. Today, He sends us to what is also a receptive harvest field. Once again, we see Him instructing the seventy-two to first demonstrate the Kingdom (heal the sick) and then to tell them "that was the Kingdom that just came to you." Some days later, the seventy-two returned with great joy, delighted that God worked through each of them to bring tangible signs of his Kingdom to people. Jesus' response to them is very interesting: He said *"I saw Satan fall like lightning."* I don't believe Jesus was saying this simply because people had been healed and set free – that had been going on for quite some time already. So what was behind these words of Jesus? The Kingdom had just multiplied again; it had gone from one representative to thirteen and now to eighty-five. Jesus knew that the Kingdom would continue to advance and that there was no going back.

In Daniel 2, the prophet sees the Kingdom of God overwhelming, in fact crushing, every other Kingdom. Isaiah says that there will be no end to the increase of this Kingdom (Isa. 9:7). God's Kingdom, unlike earthly kingdoms, starts very small like yeast or a mustard seed. But when it takes root it grows and grows. This is why for many years now I have been committed to equipping people to heal the sick and to do the works of the Kingdom and then release them as soon as possible to go out and do it themselves. On our Journeys of Compassion into the developing world we always see many hundreds and sometimes thousands of people healed. Everyone who comes on a Journey with us sees God use them to heal the sick. This is incredibly empowering in their lives, not only in the developing world but when they return home. However, when leading a Journey of Compassion I actually pray for fewer people than anyone else on the team. For over thirty years I have been thrilled to see God heal the sick; however, I am committed to releasing others and therefore I deliberately take a back seat on Journeys of Compassion. And in this way, Journey after Journey, I see more and more men, women and children connecting the power of heaven to the needs of the people in front of them. In this way I am very tangibly participating in the multiplication of God's Kingdom. Of course when I release even brand-new believers to go out and heal the sick I am aware that I am taking a risk. But if there is no release (risk), there is no multiplication of the Kingdom.

In about 640 BC the prophet Habakkuk looked across to the last days of history had declared this: *"For the earth will be filled with the knowledge of the glory of the Lord as the waters cover the sea"* (Hab. 2:14).

Never before in history has the Kingdom advanced as rapidly as it is doing now. The growth of the church worldwide is unprecedented. Modern transportation, telecommunication, and information systems allow the Gospel to be declared in ways that probably could not even have been imagined even a generation ago. So how does the "knowledge of the glory of the Lord cover the earth as the water covers the seas"? This powerful prophecy will largely be fulfilled through the multiplication of disciples; as they reach further and further, penetrating nations, people groups, remote villages, releasing the tangible reality of God's Kingdom to those who do not know Him – it is *then* that the experiential knowledge of God will cover the Earth. While describing the last days to His disciples, Jesus said this in Matthew 24: *"And this gospel of the Kingdom will be proclaimed throughout the whole world as a testimony to all nations, and then the end will come"* (Matt. 24:14 ESV). In 2 Peter 3:12 we are told that we can hasten the coming of the day the Lord. It is the sovereign God who is in control of all history. Nevertheless, in a wonderful and mysterious way, again and again He invites us to participate with Him in releasing His intentions in our world.

Having looked at *how* the Kingdom comes through men and women who are willing to leave their areas of comfort and take risks, to go wherever the Lord beckons, and to freely scatter the seeds of the gospel through both their words and actions, we are ready to look at the *why* of the Kingdom – compassion is our motivation.

5

COMPASSION: THE MOTIVATION OF THE KINGDOM

When he saw the crowds, he had compassion on them, because they were harassed and helpless, like sheep without a shepherd.   MATTHEW 9:36

In both the Old Testament and the New, God tells us again and again to watch our hearts. Right actions without right motivation accomplish nothing that will last. As we look at the Kingdom of God, it is absolutely vital that we establish the right motivation. Otherwise, as history teaches us, pursuit of the Kingdom easily leads to triumphalism and dominance; these reflect the spirit of the world, not the Spirit of Christ.

THE COMPASSIONATE JESUS

Jesus lived His entire life with a great awareness of the mission given to Him by His heavenly Father. Jesus saw His mission in the midst of the crowds of people. And His heart was continuously and deeply stirred by what He saw in their lives.

God loves people. Not *some* people. Not just Christian people.

People. He always has and He always will. The Father sent Jesus to people. The Kingdom is about God coming to people. So what motivated Jesus? *Compassion.* Day after day, in situation after situation, no matter whom He stood before, Jesus was moved with compassion. For Jesus, compassion was the foundation and motivation of all His Kingdom activity.

There are several Greek words that are translated compassion. The most common one used to describe the compassion of Jesus in His ministry is *splangchnizomai.* This is a strong word which means to be moved in one's inward parts; in other words, to feel it in your guts. When Jesus saw the sick and the oppressed He did not simply feel pity; He felt their pain Himself and this propelled Him forward. True compassion, the compassion of Jesus, always leads to action. This is *empowered compassion.* Matthew 9:36 tells us that Jesus was moved with compassion because He saw the people as distressed and downcast. These are powerful words in the original language. Distressed literally means to be harassed or molested. Downcast was a wrestling term meaning to be pinned down by force. Jesus saw the work of the enemy, the effects of the powers that be to oppress people: with sickness, pain, disease; with poverty; with conflict and strife. And when He saw them, He was moved with splangchnizomai.

Jesus felt compassion for whole groups of people: hungry crowds, the sick multitudes. He walked into villages and felt the oppression and pain that hung there. He felt compassion for the individuals whom He encountered, whether it was the outcast leper or the demonized man that everyone else feared. When Jesus saw a widow and her son's funeral procession, what motivated Him was not a desire to demonstrate the amazing power of God, but gut-wrenching compassion.

Sometimes when we are in the midst of great trials, when a loved one is sick, when we seem to be enmeshed in a situation with no way out, it is easy to feel abandoned or overlooked by the

Lord. But Jesus, who never changes, is with us *and* He is moved with compassion for us. In John 14 Jesus said, *"If you've seen me you've seen the Father."* Every action and word of Jesus reveals the heart and will of the Father. Jesus' miracles are expressions of the divine purpose of the Father. We never need doubt the Father's heart of compassion for us; and His compassion is *empowered compassion.*

For Jesus, compassion changed the atmosphere. As we walk in His rhythm, the same is true for us. When Jesus entered any situation, the possibilities changed because He brought with Him the tangible reality of the Kingdom of God. It is so important for us to remember that Jesus said, *"In the same way the Father sent Me, now I am sending you"* (John 20:21, paraphrase). That is why I spend so much time in the gospels: I want to be a life-long learner of how Jesus lived as One sent on a mission. Disciples are called to do what Jesus did, and to go where Jesus goes – and where Jesus went, things changed.

• • •

A number of years ago, I took a team from Canada to some villages in northern India. We spent two days in the village where there were a church and Bible school. The school and church had a high brick wall around them, which, in fairness, was partly a response to some very serious persecution they had experienced a few years previously. When our bus arrived in the village and we walked through the lane ways, absolutely no one would look at us. Every head was bowed down and eyes averted our gaze. There was a very heavy atmosphere in this village of several thousand. As I taught the pastors and Bible students that morning, I was deeply aware of the lethargy and prevalent lack of faith among the listeners. They believed they were in a hostile environment, again with some justification because of the past. When we encounter complacency, we are really seeing the fruit of long established fear.

While another team member taught, I slipped out of the compound and began to walk along the lane ways of the village. Every person I passed I greeted with the traditional, *"Namaste"* – a wonderful Hindi word that is loosely translated, "God in me greets God in you." Again and again there was no response – eyes were still averted and I was greeted with silence. Finally, as I passed a bench where two women sat talking, my greeting was reciprocated. When I smiled at them they immediately began to speak to me in Hindi, which of course I could not understand. Gesturing for them to wait, I ran back to the compound and got a friend of mine to translate for me. It was a simple conversation – we exchanged information about our children; I told them a little bit about Canada, and as we talked people began to gather – first the children, then the women. I could feel the atmosphere changing. I had brought back a guitar with me and so I began to sing a couple of simple songs. A few of our team members found me and joined in. Before long, the children and we were exchanging songs. A little girl began to do a dance; we joined in and in no time there were scores and scores of children dancing while the women watched and clapped. By now the men were coming and standing around the edge and watching. I taught the children a simple and universal song, "Hallelujah," which they sang beautifully. Then I told them about my friend Jesus and how He loves to heal and that He would love to heal right now. Healing is a powerful expression of the compassion of Jesus. I remember a nine- or ten-year-old boy who was brought forward by his mother. He'd been born blind in one eye. We prayed for him and immediately the Lord opened his eye, much to the delight and amazement of the village crowd.

We stayed in that village until long after dark, watching Jesus heal person after person, men and women, young and old. In the midst of it all there was great joy and celebration. The next morning our team came back for the second day of teaching at the Bible school. Same team, same bus ... but an entirely different village. As the bus came around the final bend, someone shouted out and the people began to stream forward. Before we could get out of the bus there must have been one or two hundred gathered around us. And even as we tried to walk slowly to the Bible school, smiling people were taking us by the hand – "Come into my house. Come into my house." Joy and love and warmth are universal. They need no translation. After the morning session of teaching, we went outside of the building for a short break. We were greeted by something I won't forget: a large group of children singing, "Hallelujah." It was a joyous, beautiful, holy moment.

Compassion changes the atmosphere and with it come new possibilities.

LIGHT IN THE DARKNESS
JOHN 1:5

St. Augustine called John's prologue the most sublime words ever written, and I think I would have to agree. One of my favorite verses in this passage is verse five: *"The light shines in the darkness and the darkness does not overcome it."* Notice the verse does not say the light shone *at* the darkness, or the light shone *near* the darkness, but the light shone *in* the darkness. Once again, in this verse we see Jesus, the seeking King, repeatedly running into the darkness. Even the briefest look at the Gospel account makes it apparent that Jesus would continuously go to people and be among them. His compassionate heart was completely at ease with humanity in all its expressions. People knew where to find Him: not in the synagogue or classroom, but in the marketplace, on the streets, by the lake. Jesus ran into the darkness of people's lives. He ran into dark situations because He was not afraid of the darkness. He knew He had a solution for the darkness. Jesus knew that when He encountered darkness, something was going to change – and it was *not* Him. That is why we see Jesus completely at ease among those that others referred to as "sinners," with tax gatherers, with prostitutes, with the doctrinally impure, with the ceremonially unclean, even with the demonically oppressed. In fact, it is fitting on many levels that His last hours upon this earth were spent hanging between two thieves, condemned for the severity of their crimes.

Obviously when light and darkness come together in a room, it is the darkness that flees; it does not absorb the candlelight. Yet religion so easily and so quickly forgets this. In Chapter 9 of Matthew's Gospel we see such a clear picture of this. Earlier in the day Jesus, the inviting King, says to Matthew, the tax gatherer, "You come too. Of course you are included." Whenever we encounter tax gatherers in the gospels, we are encountering broken and rejected men. Tax gatherers worked for the hated occupiers, the Romans. They were considered traitors by the Jewish people. They were social outcasts accepted only by other tax gatherers. When Jesus reached out to him, Matthew did what most people do when they encounter Jesus: he instinctively invited his friends to meet Jesus. And so we see Jesus in the midst of tax gatherers and "sinners." Jesus, "the Light," was going into the darkness.

This was more than the religious people could endure. We see them standing outside of Matthew's place, appalled and offended that Jesus would be among people like this. They thought Jesus' willingness to be among Matthew's friends disqualified him from ministry. Jesus was never threatened or felt insecure about being with Matthew's friends. We have no record that he required them to repent. Jesus knew who He was, and He knew that His nearness in and of itself had transformational power in the lives of the people around Him. Jesus knew that Matthew's friends would not change Him; just being with Jesus would change them. And that is why He told the religious people outside, *"It's not the healthy who need a doctor but the sick; I did not come for those who consider themselves righteous, but for those who know their need as sinners"*

(Matt. 9:13, paraphrase). That is why the apostle Paul said in 2 Corinthians 2:14, *"We carry with us everywhere the fragrance of Christ."* Paul is saying that because the Spirit of Christ lives in us, wherever we go we change the atmosphere. What was impossible before, now becomes possible. Jesus ran into the darkness totally secure, totally confident, and looking forward to what His Father was about to do.

My travels take me to many churches around the world every year. I am often saddened to see how few churches understand John 1:5. Too many churches are afraid of the darkness. Instead of running into the darkness, they run from it. I believe that this is because they do not know the power of the Spirit of Christ living within them. Many pastors and leaders week after week present their congregations with a very confusing message. On the one hand they encourage the members to bring the unsaved to church. On the other hand they warn them, "but stay away from those sinners. Don't let them taint you." Now if that is not a formula for confusion, I don't know what is. Paul said that clearly we are in the world but not of the world. That is because we have Christ in us – the seeking and inviting King who runs into the darkness, and who says, "You come too!"

Often when meeting with church leaders, especially in the West, I am told about all the darkness and sin in their city. It is almost as if the church is surprised and scandalized by the darkness – but isn't darkness … dark? It is interesting to me that this reaction seems to be less prevalent in the developing world's churches. My point is this: Jesus never seemed to be shocked or surprised by sin. That is because He understood that darkness is dark and sinners sin. I will write it again – Jesus ran into the darkness because of His compassion and certainty that He had the solution for the darkness.

•   •   •

Almost thirty years ago, while I was pastoring my first church in a small town, I became aware that I had very little regular contact with people outside my congregation. The men in this small town gathered at the local pool hall. They gathered to play billiards and socialize, most typically with a beer and a cigarette. The pool hall was where the men were, so if I was going to befriend them, that is where I needed to be. So I started going to the pool hall every Monday. I didn't go with the Bible in my hands or a large cross around my neck. I am sure that no one even knew I was a pastor of a small church on the edge of town. I went to shoot pool and to see what God would do. Before very many weeks I found myself listening as men poured out their worries and their pain. I heard about marriages and children, about financial strain, about job frustration. And again and again these conversations were sprinkled with words like, "I don't know why I'm telling you this. I don't talk about this stuff with anybody." I would just nod and smile and listen and let God build a bridge while they were sharing with me. These men certainly did not know me as anyone other than a guy who came every Monday night to play pool. I was not on some kind of secret mission; I was enjoying being with them. At the same time, there was a confidence in me that Christ in me would just naturally come out and change the atmosphere. I did not have to *try* to be a Christian – I already was! This is what Paul meant when he wrote in 2 Corinthians 2:14 that we carry with us everywhere the fragrance of Christ. In time, doors opened, friendships developed and an authentic bridge was built whereby I could meet some of these men and tell them about Jesus and pray for them. I remember the joy of knowing that one of them gave his life to the Lord. But I am sorry to say, the story is not over.

As I said it was my first church, and it was a conservative community. One night there was a knock on my door and I found the elders from the church standing there asking if they could come in. Perplexed, I invited them in. Immediately I sensed their frustration. "Pastor, we have heard a rumor that you have been seen playing billiards in the pool hall. Surely that isn't true is it?" Without hesitation I assured them that indeed I was there every Monday. They were very upset and insisted that if I were to remain their pastor, I would have to stop going there. I do not have very many regrets about decisions I have made in ministry over the years, but that was one of them. With sadness, but not desiring to be the source of upset or conflict in the church, I agreed to stop going to the pool hall. Jesus came "to seek and to save those that are lost." He ran into the darkness unafraid and secure in who He was and what His mission was. May I become more like Him.

BEAUTY FOR ASHES
ISAIAH 61:3

In His inaugural sermon (Luke 4:18–19), Jesus quoted the opening passage of Isaiah 61. Through this passage, Jesus declared His mission to bring good news to the poor, to set captives free and recovery of sight for the blind. The next verse in Isaiah 61 also gives us insight into Jesus' ministry: *"He gives beauty for ashes, joy for sadness, and a garment of praise for a spirit of heaviness"* (Isa. 61:3).

This describes what Jesus did when He ran into the darkness. Jesus came to heal brokenness, not to point a finger at it and certainly not to ignore it. All around Him Jesus encountered the brokenness – the ashes – of people's lives. And when He encountered these ashes, He always made an exchange, replacing the sickness and the brokenness, the isolation and despair with something beautiful. Jesus brings hope and life to the ashes of people's lives. Even a casual examination of the gospels illustrates this as Jesus, with person after person, made the exchange. A leper, not only faced with a lifelong illness but with complete social alienation, receives something beautiful from Jesus and his life is renewed forever. Blindness is exchanged for sight; deafness for hearing; muteness for speech. Shame is exchanged for forgiveness, and loneliness is exchanged for inclusion.

This is what Jesus did every day; this is the activity of the Kingdom into which He invites us. All around us are ashes, the brokenness, sickness and sadness of people's lives. They are everywhere – in the coffee shop, at work, our schools and colleges, in the supermarket, along the streets, over our backyard fences. And what do ashes sound like? The person at work who says, "I've had this headache for three days." When you overhear someone telling a friend that she has just received a bad report from her doctor, or her husband has lost his job. Maybe it is the man down the street whose wife has just passed away. As we learn to recognize the sound of ashes, we begin to understand that there are opportunities all around us every day to bring the reality of the Kingdom of God to people's lives. Like Jesus, we are called to make the exchange: beauty for ashes. Many times these exchanges are completely life altering for people.

Healing is a sign of God's Kingdom, and when His kingdom comes it always brings change. We need to see healing in a bigger paradigm than just freedom from pain or the opening of blind eyes. Once I was with friends in a town north of Manila in the Philippines, conducting a mobile medical clinic among the poor. A little seven-year-old boy brought his nine-year-old cousin to me. "This is Angelica. Since she was born she has never heard and has never spoken. Will you pray for her?" I prayed for her that morning, but no healing took place. That evening we were out on the street playing with children. To our surprise more and more of them came and before long we were a large group – all dancing and laughing and singing together. This was in an area known for drug trafficking and prostitution, but that night you would not have known it. In the midst of the laughing and dancing and singing, the Kingdom came and the atmosphere changed. There were now one to two hundred children along with a growing number of adults.

Two of my friends, recognizing that God's presence had broken in, began to use a puppet to tell these children about Jesus. "A J" the puppet, was a great evangelist. Before long almost all of the children and many of the adults were inviting Jesus into their hearts. The team then started to pray for the children and we saw the Lord immediately begin to heal many all around us. As I turned there was the little boy with his cousin Angelica. I called my puppeteer friend over and asked her to pray for this young girl. I do not think that my friend completed more than one sentence of her prayer when suddenly Angelica's eyes got large and she began to look all around her. Immediately the other children realized what had happened and began speaking, clapping their hands, snapping their fingers. Angelica heard it all. Within moments she began to speak the first words of her life. At one level we can say that she was healed and indeed she was, but I believe that something even greater happened – her life was rescued, beauty for ashes. In a moment the entire direction of her life changed; her future changed. What had been impossible for her from now on would be completely possible.

Sometimes the ashes are not so obvious and the exchange not so outwardly dramatic. But when we ask someone at work with a headache if we can pray for them and they are healed, an exchange has taken place. When we meet an elderly person sitting alone on a park bench and we take the time to listen and then to pray for them, an exchange has taken place. One day I went to a shopping center in my city to wash windshields as a simple expression of God's care and attention. While I was washing one windshield, an elderly woman who owned the car came up to me and asked what I was doing (of course!). When I explained that it was just a simple little way of reminding her how much God loved her she thanked me and then offered to give me some money. (It is interesting how in our society we do not know how to respond to acts of kindness – and no, I didn't accept her money). I carried on to the next car and the next. To my surprise, several minutes later, I turned around and saw the woman standing beside me again. She thanked me again for cleaning her windshield and once again I told her I was pleased to do it and that she was very special to God. As this gentle lady stood staring at me, I saw tears in her eyes. Quietly, but deliberately she said to me, "My husband died last month and now I am all alone." There are ashes all around us and I believe Jesus has given all of His disciples an assignment: always be prepared to exchange something beautiful for the ashes of people's lives.

COMPASSION IS ACTIVE

I suppose that if I had to choose just one verse from the Bible it would be Luke 15:20: *"But while the son was still a long way off, his father saw him and was filled with compassion for him; and he ran to his son, threw his arms around him and kissed him."* This is the pivotal point in the story that Jesus told about a lost son. This verse describes the heart of the father; it gives us a good picture of Biblical compassion – *splangchnizomai.*

First of all the father *saw* his son. Compassion is a bridge to the isolated, the harassed, the pinned down. Compassion says, "I see you. You are *not* invisible." Compassion sees what others do not see. Secondly, the father ran to his son. Compassion takes the initiative; it is active, it moves forward; it not only sees, compassion also responds. The fiery passion of Jesus beating in the hearts of His disciples is what compels us to not only see the invisible and to hear the sound of the ashes of their lives, but also it propels us forward. Like the One we are following, we run into the darkness.

In 2008 I took a team to Peru. For several days we ministered in a number of different villages that were situated against the very steep foothills outside of Lima. These houses were shanties made with cardboard and tin, dug by hand into the dirt on the side of the steep hills. To my amazement we discovered that it had not rained there since 1973. I shudder to think what would happen to these shanties if there were ever a sudden downpour – hundreds of them would be swept to the valley in just moments. While the medical clinic that we were conducting was going on in the town below, some of us climbed the steep hills to greet and pray for those who lived in the various shanties.

We saw God do many wonderful miracles. I remember the complete healing of an elderly woman who had been paralyzed on one side for seven years because of a stroke. I will never forget the sight of her looking with amazement at her arm and leg is she continued to move them about. We also saw blind eyes open, tumors disappear, fevers leave. But perhaps the thing I remember most about that afternoon was what one of our team members shared with me. As his team reached one of the houses perched precariously on the side of the hill and offered to pray with the woman who lived there, she told him that she had been in her home for over four years and that this was the first time that anyone had ever come to her door. After the team prayed for this woman and they began to move on to the next house, my friend could not help but look down to the church below where the clinic was going on. In over four years, no one had come to see this woman. The compassion of Jesus sees the invisible.

In Luke 10 Jesus told the parable of the good Samaritan. This is one of the most challenging stories He ever told because it takes us from theory to practice. Jesus told this story in response to a man who was trying to avoid his responsibility to the Lord's command to love his neighbor by complicating the issue with the question, "Well that is all fine, but really, who *is* my neighbor?" This is a story that challenges our priorities. A man is beaten, robbed and left for dead on the side of the Jericho road. A priest walks by on the other side of the road, as does the Levite. Finally, a Samaritan sees the man, stops and helps him by dressing his wounds and carrying him to a place where the man can recover. This is perhaps Jesus'

best-known parable, but one filled with an irony that would have
been immediately apparent to his first century Jewish audience.

This is a story about awareness. The Jericho road was
seventeen miles long and went through some of the most rugged
and dangerous territory in all of Israel. But (and here is the irony),
the Jericho road was only eight feet wide. It would have taken
some effort for the priest and the Levite to walk past the wounded
man. The second point of irony in this story is the identity of the
third traveler. In our day the modern listener hears Samaritan
and thinks of somebody who is good. But in first century Israel,
Samaritans were mistrusted and avoided by the Jews. For hundreds
of years they had lived as a separate and "mixed race" people. This
mixture was apparent in their religious beliefs; over the centuries
a variety of beliefs from other religions and cultures had blended
with the Jewish faith. So when Jesus identified a third traveler as a
good Samaritan it was meant to shock and challenge His listeners'
assumptions. Perhaps the closest we, as Christians, could come
to experiencing the impact today would be to speak of perhaps
the good Mormon or maybe even the good Muslim. The point is
that it was the traveler demonstrating compassion and mercy who
reflected the heart of the Father. He saw the wounded man at the
side of the road and made a choice to get involved. Compassion
is not a feeling; biblical compassion always leads to involvement.
Thirdly we see that this cost the Samaritan in time, convenience and
money. For the first three centuries of its existence, the church was
known for its active compassion even by its enemies. Historical
records tell us that even during times of Roman persecution, the
Romans respected the church for their care for widows, orphans
and the poor.

Biblical compassion, the compassion into which Jesus calls
us, is costly. It challenges our priorities. At a time when North
Americans spend more money each year on male baldness remedies
than the entire estimated cost of eliminating the number one health

issue in the developing world – the problem of unsafe drinking water – disciples of Jesus must embrace biblical compassion. At a time when over thirty thousand children die from totally preventable causes every day, we must choose the awareness and active involvement of the compassion of Jesus.

There is an emotional cost to compassion as well. If we are willing to go to the poor and the broken and the sick, if we are willing to stop for the one who is lying on the side of the road, at times we will fight feeling overwhelmed. Many times we will need to remember that Jesus puts the wounded one on the side of the road in our lives because our Lord knows He has given us what we need in order to minister to that one.

Not long ago I was walking through a very poor village in Central America. For five months I had been traveling in Africa, India and the Philippines. I had been in too many poor rural villages and urban slums to count. Yes, I had seen thousands of people come to Jesus and thousands healed of various diseases and afflictions. But all of this had taken place in the midst of such abject poverty. I had seen so much systemic injustice. Now, as I walked in this poor Nicaraguan barrio, suddenly I felt overwhelmed by what I was seeing yet again. I was tired and frustrated. At that moment, it was all too much. Suddenly I sensed the compassionate presence of Jesus. I said out loud, "Jesus, this isn't too much for you. Your heart is big enough for all of these people and all of the villages and all of the people I've been to this year – and all of the villages and towns in the whole world." This was not theology, it was a sudden and deep understanding of the inclusive, compassionate love of Jesus for everyone, and of the miraculous power of the cross.

COMPASSION AND ME

For over three years Jesus ministered in an area of only about forty by seventy miles. Yet when we consider that He traveled by foot and, according to the historian Josephus, the area encompassed about two hundred towns with a total population of perhaps two million people, it is hard to really grasp the outside pressures exerted upon Him. However, in the midst of the almost endless demands, and of being confronted daily by the pain of people's lives, Jesus never lost His deep compassion, His ability to care for and about the person standing in front of Him.

No one would argue the merit and importance of living with compassion, especially as we seek to live as disciples of the Compassionate One. However, under the pressure of busy schedules and others' expectations, we are left living with the dynamic tension created by the gap between our intentions and our lives. Like Paul, we are left to cry out, *"I want to do what is right, but I can't. I want to do what is good, but I don't"* (Rom. 7:18–19 NLT). As a "Type A" person, I may be more prone to this than some others, but if I let myself be driven by my goals and agendas, it is so easy for me to see people as obstacles rather than as gifts to be valued. There is a great difference between completing tasks and being motivated to produce fruit that reveals and celebrates the goodness of the Father (John 15:8).

In certain circumstances, with particular individuals, I can feel and demonstrate at least some degree of the compassion, the splangchnizomai, that Jesus demonstrated, but usually only to those people whose behavior naturally draws out sympathy and understanding. It is hard for me to find compassion for those with whom I feel no affinity or affection. And what about those who offend me? Forget it. There is no compassion for the one who gets angry with me on the road, or the parent I hear yelling at their child in the store or restaurant. What about those who themselves seem to be so unfeeling and insensitive? The best I can do is to remind myself that as a Christian, I *should* be compassionate. And so I am left with either feeling guilty because I don't feel anything like that, or with my backup position: pretending to feel something that

I really don't. (I think Jesus called this hypocrisy – ouch!)

There are two main things that seem to keep me from living the compassionate, inclusive life of Jesus that truly feels the pain of others. Firstly, I allow myself to get too busy; busyness always leads me to self-focused living. Secondly, I so often take the easy route of not seeing past the surface behavior of people to the pain and wounding that is at its root. How different my life would be, how different our churches would be, if we could see past people's hard exterior, past their veneer of callousness and abrasiveness, and begin to see them as they really are – molested and pinned down.

Jesus said that a little yeast, though tiny and almost invisible, when it comes into contact with its surroundings, eventually permeates and changes its environment. As we are willing to let God first confront, then change us, into seeking, inviting and compassionate people, *this* will change our communities. For the first three hundred years of its existence, the early church embraced radical compassion; doing this was financially and socially very costly, but it proved that indeed Jesus was right – His new community of empowered compassion changed the very structure of the Roman world. Jesus continues to cry out over His church: *"Go figure out what this Scripture means: 'I'm after mercy, not religion"* (Matt. 9:13 MSG). An uncomfortable reality for the twenty-first century church in the West is that most outsiders can only identify Christians by two issues: we are the people who hate gays and are against abortion. Is this the full scope of the message that Jesus' words and actions demonstrated in Israel?

HOW DO I BEGIN TO EXPERIENCE THE SPLANGCHNIZOMAI OF JESUS?

Before I am asked to show compassion toward the distressed and downcast, the molested and pinned down, even before I am asked to show compassion to brothers and sisters in their pain, Jesus first invites me to accept His compassion in *my* life. Embracing the inviting, accepting compassion of Jesus is deeply transformative. This takes me back to the first blessing of the Sermon on the Mount: *"Blessed are the poor in spirit, for theirs is the kingdom of the heavens."* This is a grace-filled promise. I am not blessed by God *because* I am poor in spirit, but in spite of it. In the midst of my brokenness and failure, He says, "Even in this, you are blessed by Me." When the prodigal son was embraced and kissed by his father, he had only one thing to do: receive the homecoming. He did not try to cut it short. He did not do anything but experience the compassion and welcome of his father. Frankly, this takes faith. Since we do not naturally live out of a paradigm of compassion, it is difficult for us to receive it. Paul Tillich famously said that, "Faith is the courage to accept acceptance."[5] The degree of our compassion for others seems to depend in large part upon our capacity for believing and living in the acceptance that Christ has for us. In an era when bookshelves are filled with how to be self-accepting, two thousand years of devotional and theological consideration teach us that self-acceptance which is not based upon the sacrificial and passionate acceptance of Jesus is too difficult to hold onto because it relies on us and not Him. Without a life rooted in the Lord's compassion and acceptance, when confronted with our inconsistencies and failures, we easily fall into disappointment and frustration with ourselves. When I am most unhappy with myself, I am most critical of others; when I am most self-condemning, I am most judgmental of the motives and actions of those around me.

Jesus has given us a wonderful key to moving from self-criticism to living in the confidence and deep contentment of His acceptance. It is found in John 15, one of the richest chapters in all of scripture:

"I am the true vine; my Father is the gardener. He cuts

5 Paul Tillich, *The Shaking of the Foundations* (New York: Charles Scribner's Sons, 1948), 42.

off every branch of mine that does not produce fruit. And
he trims and cleans every branch that produces fruit so
that it will produce even more fruit. You are already clean
because of the words I have spoken to you. Remain in me,
and I will remain in you. A branch cannot produce fruit
alone but must remain in the vine. In the same way, you
cannot produce fruit alone but must remain in me.

"I am the vine, and you are the branches. If any remain
in me and I remain in them, they produce much fruit. But
without me they can do nothing" (John 15:1–6 NCV).

Although there are numerous themes to pursue in this passage, the
key to a change of attitude and behavior is a change of internal
motivation – the core values from which we live. Jesus is giving
His disciples keys for living from their center, where He is with
them. First, Jesus reminds His friends that the challenges they face,
including being confronted with their own failures, are reflections
of the work of their heavenly Father in pruning and refining
them. (It is interesting that in the original language, "prune" can
be translated "clean.") When people come against us, instead of
instinctively seeing them as our enemy, Jesus is telling us that God
is using them for His loving work in our lives. Secondly, when
we start to feel overwhelmed with our failures, He tells us that we
are already clean. This is how He sees us. This is the wonder of
the work of the cross. It reminds us of the Shulamite woman in
the Song of Solomon who said, "I am dark, yet lovely!" When we
feel overwhelmed by our sin, our Father says, "No. I say you are
beautiful, because that is how I see you in My Son." Jesus lived
with a deep sense of His own acceptance by the Father. He invites
us to the same. Thirdly, Jesus tells us the key to fruitful living:
times of intimacy with Him. But He goes further: without a life
built on intimacy with Him, it is impossible for our lives to produce
enduring fruit. This includes the fruit of authentic, empowering
compassion. In His Great Commandment, Jesus said that all of

scripture is summed up in two things – love God and love people. They are interrelated, not separate. True devotion (loving God) must always lead us to a right ethic (loving people). Conversely, the challenges of loving people will always bring us to the end of ourselves and push us back to true devotion.

This intimacy and daily dependency on the compassion of God is the key to maturity. The Father's goal for us, according to Romans 8:29, is to be molded into the image of Jesus. Contrary to the focus of many modern day discipleship programs, the example of Jesus demonstrated that mature saints are not the most self-controlled; they are the most loving and compassionate. We need leadership according to Jesus' standard: *"I'm after mercy, not religion"* (Matt. 9:13 MSG).

JOURNAL ENTRY: PICTURES FROM INDIA

The team is leaving now, going back to their various cities and towns in the UK, US and Canada. Once again, it is hard to imagine that we have not all known each other for years; I never cease to wonder at how God joins people's hearts so quickly and deeply in the midst of Kingdom activity. As always, saying goodbye is bitter-sweet. Christina and I remain for two days, then off to Australia for a tour of conferences and meetings.

For now, just a few memories and images from the past two weeks.

While driving in the vans to feed the beggars around the railway station, we see a man half-naked lying still on the sidewalk. I think he is dead. Vince jumps out of the van and goes over to check on him. There is a filthy blanket nearby – more a rag really – that he covers the man with. He is mostly unconscious and trembling. So little to be done in the midst of overwhelming poverty that I have no words to describe. Yet Vince's simple gesture touches my heart deeply. Mother Teresa was so right when she said that we can do no great things, only small things with great love.

• • •

Sunday evening. Vince's team has worked for weeks for this moment: a concert on the beach in the center of the city. As the band plays the people gather. Then Ken and Deb begin to sing. I had no idea how talented they are, how much stage presence they carry. Now the crowd surges forward. The young ones begin to dance and shout, waving their arms to the beat of the music. In a few minutes there are over 10,000 people. The traffic on the main road that runs alongside the beach is stopped as people get out of their cars to listen. The energy is palpable, electric. After some time, Vince and I address the crowd. They are really listening. We finish with an invitation to pray with us to ask Christ into their lives. Then we ask those who prayed that for the first time and from their hearts to raise their hands. Hands everywhere, thousands of them. The Impact team prays for hundreds. More salvations; people sharing with the team their deepest hurts. We leave thankful, but deeply moved.

•   •   •

(From a rural village)

We have treated many hundreds of sick people in the mobile clinic today. After an hour of rest, we are standing in the middle of this village of about 2,000. It is 6 p.m. From all over the village, the people begin to gather, drawn by the music. Loud music, dance, some great songs from Ken & Deb (who are amazing!). After some testimonies of healings that had occurred that day, I begin to tell them about Jesus. There are at least 500 gathered and listening attentively – almost all of them Hindus. When I invite them to come forward and give their lives to Jesus, they respond immediately. With a quiet and determined eagerness, they come and they come. My first guess is that about 200 received Christ, but after talking with the team and finding out how many more they led to the Lord while praying for their illnesses, the number is likely closer to 300. Vince's remarkable team keeps getting all their names and contact info so that they will be followed up on during the coming days.

•   •   •

(From a children's prison. Children as young as three years old are gathered from the streets, or parents drop them off and abandon them. Most will not leave the prison until they are eighteen).

About fifty of the boys from the prison gather outdoors, sitting on blankets as we sing songs, do skits and generally try to bring some joy. Danielle is incredible, leading them in songs and impromptu games that she makes up on the spot. Everywhere, I see smiles. Yet as I look just thirty feet away, I see the twenty foot high prison walls rising ominously. Many of these children have no memory of life on the outside; they don't know who their parents are, or if they have siblings. Now two boys jump up and run into a building. In moment they emerge with a large box. They now have something to show us. It is a magic show. Some of the tricks are simply charming; to my surprise, others are mystifying. All the boys cheer their friends on wildly; so do we. Somehow in the midst of this prison, in the midst of profound abandonment, the boys find some joy, some pleasure. What a lesson for us all.

• • •

The final medical clinic is now over. The tents are being taken down for the last time; the meds are being counted and sorted. We are preparing for a final gathering in a church with the Impact team and the Friends Meet team. I go back to the tent to find my friend so that we can look at a piece of land for a few minutes. Coming around the corner, I am momentarily confused by what I see. There he is with another team member and the Hindu doctor who has served so diligently for all six clinics. Then I understand: he is leading the doctor to Jesus. Something about this final salvation, after seeing perhaps three thousand or more come to the Lord over these past two weeks touches me deeply. The faithfulness of our wonderful Savior.

There will be time for more writing, more reporting; but right now I simply want to savor the memories.

6

THE HEALING JOURNEY

"Heal me, O LORD, and I will be healed." JEREMIAH 17:14

From the beginning of this section on healing, I want to acknowledge a few of those who most influenced and helped me to grow in this area of ministry. I first encountered John Wimber in the mid-1980s. I was deeply impacted by his teaching, which explained the ministry of healing in the context of the breaking in of God's Kingdom upon the earth. John taught so many of us that the Kingdom is near and therefore, healing is possible here and now. Another great influence on me in the area of healing ministry has been Bob Brasset. From Bob I learned two great lessons: healing is easy because Jesus has already done the work. Secondly, I learned to pray for healing with confidence expressed through very short prayers that are directed specifically at the person's sickness or pain. As I applied what Bob taught I immediately saw a great increase in healing. Another person who has encouraged me in the area of healing is Randy Clark. I have known Randy since 1994 (for many years we were both Vineyard pastors). Several years ago I traveled with Randy to India and was greatly impacted by his teaching on the ministry of healing and on the evangelistic power of the spiritual gift of the word of knowledge.

I have been amazed and blessed at God's grace to me in healing ministry. Over the past several years I have had the privilege and great delight to teach many thousands of people how to heal the sick in Jesus' name. A number of years ago I made the decision to never teach about healing without following it immediately with the opportunity for every listener to personally participate in healing the sick. I am deeply aware that I am experiencing a harvest that these men and others sowed into my life.

GOD'S INTENTION

There are a great many excellent books that have been written about the subject of healing; the intent of this book is not to fully develop what the Scriptures say regarding this subject. However, I want to very briefly highlight a few verses since God's Word is the foundation for all that we do.

In order to step out with confidence as we begin to pray for the sick, we must get rid of all uncertainty regarding God's will in this matter. If we do not know that it is always the desire of God to heal the sick, then when we stand before someone who is sick we find ourselves inevitably asking, "Father, do you want to heal this one?" To be effective in healing, it is imperative that we move from hoping God will heal to knowing that He will.

God's will is perfectly revealed in His Word. In Exodus 15:26, God reveals one of His covenant names to Moses: "I am the Lord who heals you." Who He is (Jehovah Rapha) expresses His promise to His people. A few years ago I spoke at a church in Paris. As I walked into the building I was delighted to see a huge banner stretched across the front of the church: *"Praise the Lord, O my soul, and forget not all his benefits – who forgives all your sins and heals all your diseases"* (Psa. 103:2–3). Could any promise be clearer? Healing is not so much about who we are and what we think, as it is about who God is and what He says. *"He sent His Word and healed them"* (Psa. 107:20 NASB). *"All the promises of God are Yes, and in Him, Amen to the glory of God through us"* (2 Cor. 1:20 NKJ).

In the remarkable "Suffering Servant" prophecy of Isaiah

53, the prophet looks across hundreds of years and sees the crucifixion of Jesus. In the midst of this powerful passage Isaiah writes,

> *Surely He took up our infirmities and carried our sorrows, yet we considered Him stricken by God, smitten by Him, and afflicted. But He was pierced for our transgressions, He was crushed for our iniquities, the punishment that brought us peace was upon Him, and by His wounds we are healed"* (Isa. 53:4-5).

At the cross Jesus paid for both our sin and our sickness. As He hung on the cross He said, "It is finished"; it was a complete work with nothing else required. This is why I tell people that fundamentally, healing is easy because Jesus already paid for it. From us to the cross goes our sin and sickness; from the cross to us comes our salvation and healing. Jesus bore my sin so that I could be free from its power. He bore my sickness by His wounds so that I could be well. Healing is to our body what salvation is to our souls. Jesus paid the ultimate price for our healing that only He could pay. This is so important for us to grasp. On the times when I feel too tired, too discouraged, too busy, and I am tempted not to pray for the sick – those are the times I remember that we pray for the sick so that Jesus can have what He already bought and paid for.

THE KINGDOM AND HEALING

The Kingdom of God is an all-encompassing Kingdom which brings with it new possibilities. The Kingdom is not an idea or concept – it comes with tangible signs. The good news embraces new economic opportunity, freedom from oppression, medical care, reconciliation, and supernatural healing. When the reality of heaven touches people's bodies, causing pain and sickness to disappear, this is a tangible sign that God's Kingdom is in their midst. This is the gospel that Jesus preached and demonstrated;

this is the gospel that He has entrusted to us.

Healing is much more than the leaving of pain or sickness from someone's body. Healing is the result of a greater reality breaking in – the Kingdom of the heavens suddenly comes and begins to change what is really a lesser reality: our condition on earth. The power of the future overshadows the present. Jesus challenged his friends to recognize the presence of the future, the imminence of the heavens. Pain and sickness go, yes; but beyond this, when the Kingdom comes, the very atmosphere changes and with it, the possibilities.

Jesus began His Sermon on the Mount by declaring blessings and promises that were universal. Similarly, God's work of healing is offered to all who will receive it, since healing is but one sign of the presence of His Kingdom. Repeatedly, I have watched whole villages change when someone is healed. Hostility and mistrust evaporate. As the atmosphere changes, the reality of the Kingdom increases. There is an expectation that God has come to do more; and in this atmosphere, He does much more. I cannot possibly count the number of villagers that greeted me with suspicion and even antagonism, that a couple of hours later, after the Kingdom of the heavens had broken in, now followed me out of the village with smiles, songs and even dancing. Perhaps even more significantly, by opening up the hearts of the villagers to the goodness of God and His Kingdom, healing often opens doors for other long-term Kingdom activities. In an atmosphere of trust, we can work alongside the village and its leaders in bringing ongoing transformation like clinics, small farms, and micro-credit – the *"Good News to the poor"* (Matt. 11:5) that Jesus identified as a sign of the Kingdom. Everyone, everywhere was created for the greater reality of the Kingdom of God.

One of the factors that keeps believers from a lifestyle of praying for the sick is that we have too small a healing paradigm. To begin with, Jesus did not call us to heal pain and sickness, but to heal people. After an evening of seeing the Lord move through us to heal hundreds of people, it is all too easy to think in terms of conditions healed rather than lives that were changed and rescued. When a man's crippled arm is healed, his life is changed. Now he can once again work and thereby support his family. When a child suddenly begins to hear, we can say that her ears were healed; however, when we understand that the Kingdom of the heavens has broken in, we realize that God has come to rescue a whole life. The child's future has profoundly changed, including new possibilities for education, friendships, and a transformed self-image.

One of the great joys of taking people to the nations to release Kingdom activity is to see how being used by the Lord changes *us*. When we see the Lord healing through us, our understanding of who we really are begins to grow. Not many of us, after being used to heal scores or even hundreds of people over a period of two weeks, will go back home to live out a passive Christianity. Jesus encouraged the multiplication of the Kingdom through involving an ever-increasing number of people. So now, as a direct result of their experience of being used daily to heal, there are men and women actively engaged in healing ministry in their home cities in North America, Europe and Australia. Likewise, the Kingdom continues to advance in many of the villages, towns and cities in the developing world where Impact Nations has trained and released people to continue on after we have left.

As I write this, the main news story is the famine and violence in Somalia that have driven over a half million desperate people to walk for days across the desert to the refugee camp in Dadaab, Kenya. It is a terrible place with little food or water, no electricity and unrelenting heat. Dadaab is now estimated to be the largest refugee camp in the world, with fifteen thousand people being added weekly. It is also the place where, in 2005, we took a team to train hundreds of believers. We taught them about the Kingdom of God and about how to heal the sick in Jesus' name. I was told that we were the first Christian group that was permitted to hold outdoor healing and evangelism meetings in this ninety-seven percent Muslim camp. God showed up powerfully every day with amazing healing. Many turned to Jesus. But our purpose was for more than that. We worked with them to set up an ongoing healing prayer center. Every time I am confronted on my television with the images of pain, fear and desperation, I remember that the Lord knew what was coming and so in His mercy, He opened a door for us all those years ago so that now there is a place of healing and hope. The light is shining in the darkness.

Healing is not only an expression of God's compassion for the sick; it is a sign that God is actively at work. Healing awakens a new awareness and hunger for God in those who witness it. In the book of Acts again and again we see that as the apostles healed the sick many turned to Christ. This is why we see Peter and John, Philip and Stephen, Paul and Barnabas not only declaring the truth of the Kingdom, but also demonstrating it through healing and miracles.

In John 10:38, Jesus said to the people, *"If you can't believe what I'm telling you, that's okay. Believe in the miracles that you see because they point to who I really am"* (paraphrase). In 2009 I took an Impact team to some very remote villages on the island of Mindanao in the Philippines, accompanied by the army. We were in an area with a lot of terrorist activity, but with three hundred soldiers, I don't think I have ever been safer in my life! Each day we traveled by jeep, army truck and even riverboat to isolated communities, conducting the first mobile medical clinics they had ever had. In each place we shared and demonstrated the gospel. This was a wonderful opportunity and adventure. I think I will always remember the sight of forty soldiers (still holding their M16's) as they prayed and asked Jesus into their lives.

In one of these villages while the medical clinic was going on, I went with the translator to some of the houses, offering to pray for any needs. Almost immediately I was invited into a house where they brought an elderly lady to me for prayer. They explained to me that she could no longer see or hear and that she had a lot of pain in her body (which I presumed was arthritis). Jesus loves to heal and that is exactly what He did that morning. In just a few minutes she could see and hear clearly again. Then I prayed for the pain in her body and she excitedly declared that it was all gone. It was only at this point that I noticed three teenage girls standing outside, looking in the open doorway. After another couple of minutes with Lola (an affectionate term for elderly women in the Philippines), I went outside to talk to the girls. By now there were at least twenty of them standing there. I began to share the gospel with them but I could see that it was not having a lot of impact. Then I remembered John 10:38 – *"Believe in miracles because they point to Me"* (paraphrase). I asked the teenagers, "How many of you believe that Lola could not see or hear?" Her condition was common knowledge in the village and so of course they all agreed. Then I asked for Lola to come out and tell them what Jesus had just done for her. All the while more and more teenagers gathered. Now there was an openness and attentiveness to the gospel and in just a few moments I had the delight of leading the entire group – about forty young people – to Jesus.

Healing is one of the central activities in the Kingdom of God. It is also a key portion of our inheritance. Jesus gave us authority to heal in His name. I am convinced that it is available to every Christian. That is why, nearly thirty years ago, from the time they were pre-school age, I began to take my children with me to watch, learn and pray for the sick. Healing the sick is part of normal Christianity; as disciples of Jesus, it is part of our inheritance *and* our responsibility (albeit a delightful one).

MY FIRST STEPS

The first time I remember praying for healing was back in 1977. It was one of those situations that I fell into and I could not figure out how to get out of, short of simply refusing. If this doesn't sound like I was walking in a lot of faith, then you should have heard my frightened, small little prayer. After saying this rather confused, almost incomprehensible prayer with a room full of people staring at me, something amazing happened – the woman was completely healed! Not only was her pain gone but also, the next day X-rays confirmed what the Lord had done. I felt so confident and encouraged by this that I went right out and prayed for someone else – in 1983! (Well, it's not good to rush these things.) Again, as I was about to pray for a neighbor's child with hydrocephalus, it was as if my brain suddenly shut down – I couldn't seem to put three words together. The boy's parents looked at me with something less than a lot of confidence in what they had just witnessed, and I made a speedy retreat. A few days later, the doctors informed them that their son's condition had totally disappeared. By the way, to my knowledge they never gave their hearts to the Lord, but they told their neighbors what happened, and *they* came to Jesus!

A year later, I attended a conference on healing. The speaker challenged us that if we would pray for two hundred people for healing, we would never stop. Having prayed for two people in seven years, I quickly did the math and thought that at my present rate I would not live long enough to pray for two hundred people; so responding to his invitation seemed safe enough. But as I went forward, suddenly I sensed the Spirit of God all around me, and I knew that this was a holy moment and a very serious commitment that I was making. It was a turning point. Of course, I had no idea that I was embarking on the greatest adventure of my life.

God is full of mystery. St. Augustine said that if we understand God, then He is not God. There is so much that I do not understand about healing. Many times I have wondered why a person did not get healed; sometimes I have been tempted to ask why someone *did* get healed. But I do know this – I am on a journey that continues to take me, step by faltering step, into greater effectiveness in healing. The past ten years have been a significant growing time for me, and it seems that a few themes or principles are emerging.

EXPECTATION

When we settle the issue that disciples do what Jesus did, that we are called to bring the Kingdom – heaven's reality – to the people around us, then we enter into a very positive cause and effect cycle. There are challenges and disappointments, but if we keep going, before too long, we begin to see increase. And in the final analysis it cannot be otherwise because the Kingdom is always increasing. *"His ruling authority will grow, and there'll be no limits to the wholeness he brings"* (Isa. 9:7 MSG).

As we see the Lord use us to heal more powerfully and more often, something naturally begins to take root in our hearts. Confidence begins to rise up in us. This is not pride in our ability; it is a sureness that God moves through His sons and daughters to minister to the needs of hurting people. Sometimes we confuse confidence with pride. Years ago, I heard this definition of spiritual authority: confidence without arrogance; humility without apology. That is why the New Testament writers so often encouraged God's church to walk with confidence.

> *This is the confidence we have in approaching God: that if we ask anything according to his will, he hears us. 15 And if we know that he hears us – whatever we ask – we know that we have what we asked of him* (1 John 5:14–15).

> *So do not throw away your confidence; it will be richly rewarded* (Heb. 10:35).

Faith is the currency of the Kingdom. Without it, we cannot please our Master (Heb. 11:6). Jesus said many times that our faith determines what happens. We are back to the amazing truth that

God chooses to move through His kids. It is the Father's children who can release His blessing. The only way we can do it is through exercising our faith. In Mark 4, Jesus tells us not to hide the proclamation and demonstration of the Good News. He says that to have good news and to keep quiet about it is nonsensical – it would be like lighting a lamp and then hiding it. In this context he says something very interesting in Mark 4:24: *"With the measure you use, it will be used to you to you – and even more"* (TNIV). I believe that He is telling us that, in the economy of the Kingdom, whose currency is *faith*, what you expect is what you get; in fact, you get more of it. And here is that positive cause and effect cycle again. Because we see more healing, we *expect* to see more healing; therefore, we see even more healing, which causes us to expect even more. Before long, we are genuinely surprised if people are not healed when we pray for them.

I want to be very clear at this point. I am not saying that every one I (or you) pray for is always healed. But I am saying that as we see the increase which comes with confidence that our Father is moving through us, and then stand before a person who is sick or in pain, we sincerely expect God to heal.

Besides our experience, why do we expect God to move? First of all, we know who God is. He loves to heal. In fact, I am convinced that God desires to heal *all the time*. Our healing journey involves us learning how to increasingly move in rhythm with Him and how to remove any obstacles on our part. God not only loves to heal, He *is* healing. One of His covenant names that He revealed to Israel is Jehovah Rapha, "the LORD who heals you." The Bible is full of His promises to *"heal your diseases"* (Psa. 103:3) and there are many excellent books dedicated to this powerful truth that God always desires to heal.

Secondly, we can expect the Lord to heal through us because of who we are – sons and daughters of the King. We know that we have been commissioned by Jesus and empowered by the Holy

Spirit to do the works of the Father. We looked at this in an earlier chapter, but as a reminder, Jesus came to do the work of His Father. *"My Father is always at his work to this very day, and I, too, am working"* (John 5:17). *"My food,"* said Jesus, *"is to do the will of him who sent me and to finish his work"* (John 4:34). When we begin to pray for a sick or injured person, we can do so with the confident knowledge that we are "about our Father's business."

Expectation is closely linked with faith, but perhaps not in the way we think. Truthfully, I often find the hardest people to pray healing for are Christians, especially those from the Western church. The reason is often that they carry an anxiety about having enough faith. This seems to shut them down to receive; they are more focused on their perceived lack of faith, than on the mercy and faithfulness of a Father who wants to heal them. After all, Jesus said that all we need is faith the size of a mustard seed – and most of us have at least that much.

Jesus recognized faith from three sources. Often He saw faith in the person who needed to be healed. There are many examples of this – the woman suffering from bleeding, the leper, and the immoral woman who needed her heart healed. When blind Bartimaeus was brought to Jesus, his need was obvious to everyone, yet He asked the man, "What do you want?" Bartimaeus' answer both expressed and released faith, which increased his expectation in what was about to happen. The Roman Centurion only needed Jesus to speak a word of healing; he was that confident of His power to heal his servant. The Centurion's faith was so strong that it amazed Jesus.

A few years ago I was with the team in Seoul, Korea. The Lord was healing people all over the room and in this atmosphere of great faith someone brought me to a middle-aged man. The man told me that he had liver cancer and in three days he would be undergoing surgery to try to save his life. Because of the obvious life and death circumstances, I began to pray for this man with a lot of energy and fervor. But after only a few moments he reached out and touched my arm saying, "Thank you. You can stop praying now. The Lord has healed me." Given the dire circumstances facing him, I was amazed at this man's assured faith. Just six weeks later I found myself back in Korea speaking in a Presbyterian church. Before the service I met with the senior pastor and was greatly surprised when he asked me if I remembered praying for the man with liver cancer. I was in an entirely different part of the city and I had no idea that he attended this particular church. My surprise immediately turned to joy when the pastor said to me, "After you prayed for him he insisted on another scan before the surgery. They found absolutely no trace of cancer. He is completely healed."

The faith of another can increase the atmosphere for healing. When the paralytic was lowered through the roof, Jesus saw the faith of *his friends*. When the Roman centurion asked Jesus to just speak the healing word and his servant would be healed, Jesus marveled at his faith. I have often seen the power of a relative's or friend's faith to release healing, even when the sick person seemingly had no faith. When praying for the sick, we need to pay close attention to the faith atmosphere that such friends carry. Remember, faith is the currency of the Kingdom.

A couple of years ago, my wife and I were speaking at a healing conference in Canada. After one session, a lady came and asked us to please come with her to a back room to pray for her sick friend. When we entered the room, we saw a woman lying on a cot in a very late stage of cancer. She was too weak to speak; her body was incredibly emaciated. Truthfully, there seemed to be no indication that this poor woman had any great faith. But her friend had enough faith to arrange to have her transported to the meeting and to declare to my wife and me her supreme confidence that when we prayed, God would heal her friend. We prayed and at that time we could see no outward manifestation of healing. This faithful friend was not deterred in the least. She declared that God had done the healing. And that is exactly what happened. She contacted us several weeks later and told us that the woman was completely healed; there was no cancer and her body had returned to strength and vitality. A faithful friend indeed.

Sometimes faith will suddenly rise up in the person that God is about to use. One day Jesus was at the pool of Bethesda. John tells us that there were a great number of disabled people lying there, including a man who had been an invalid for thirty-eight years. Suddenly faith rose up in Jesus as He went to this one man in the midst of so many. It is interesting that like Bartimaeus, Jesus asked him if he wanted to get well – once again, He was drawing faith and expectation out of the man. In an instant, he was well. Likewise Peter, on his way to the temple, saw a lame beggar and suddenly faith rose up in him. Although we are always available to release the Kingdom, there seem to be certain moments when the Spirit stirs great faith in us, increasing our expectation that the Lord is about to do something special.

There is something else about faith: it needs to be activated. Again, the momentum of the gospel is that the Word becomes flesh. James writes at length about the relationship between faith and works; in fact, thirteen times, in as many verses (Jas. 2:14–26) he reinforces that for faith to mean anything, for it to accomplish the purposes of the Father, it must be walked out. In Luke 6 we see how Jesus brings a man with a shriveled hand into this activation. In the obviously hostile environment (ironically) of the synagogue where the leaders did not want Jesus to heal anyone, He told the man to stand up. Then He told him to walk to the front. I believe that this took significant courage on this man's part; he knew that excommunication was a real possibility. Finally, Jesus told him to stretch out his hand. Only this man could activate his faith; no one, not even Jesus could do it for him. Often, in the healing process this is the great dividing line, the moment of truth. What we really believe is reflected in our actions. And healing requires activation.

In 2005, I was a team member with Randy Clark on the east

coast of India. One night, in a gathering of over fifty thousand people, I stood in front of a woman with a severely withered arm. There appeared to be no muscle and she had to hold her arm up with her other hand. She laid her arm on the top of a fence rail that stood between us. After I prayed, commanding life to flow into her arm, releasing the power of heaven, I asked her to take her arm off the rail and move it. She looked down at an arm that was still shriveled and said, "But I can't. My arm doesn't work." I replied that what she said was true a few moments ago, but God has now healed her. She needed to activate her faith by moving her arm off that rail. She smiled at me, but I could see a lot of apprehension in her eyes. However, she stepped back and let her arm come off the rail. Instantly, life and strength flowed into her arm, increasing it to full size. She began to swing her arm over her head and all around, the whole time shouting to everyone around that she had been healed. The healing was there, waiting for her faith to be activated – something only she could do.

The principle of faith and expectation is the foundation for some other keys that seem to be connected to seeing a wonderfully increased effectiveness in praying for the sick.

ALERTNESS

Pray at all times and on every occasion in the power of the Holy Spirit. Stay alert" (Eph. 6:18 NLT).

We are surrounded by heavenly activity. The Lord is always speaking (after all, He *is* the Word), and heaven is always waiting to break into this realm. The problem is that we are often so inattentive. When Jesus announced repeatedly that the Kingdom of heaven is here, He literally was saying, "The Kingdom of the heavens is brought near to you." Jesus was saying, "The Kingdom is now all around you, like the atmosphere. From now on, you have access to the reality of the Kingdom, and that activity surrounds you." It is available, but we have to be attuned to it.

When we are really living in expectation of the breaking in of heaven, this anticipation always leads to an alertness – and alertness quickens our senses. Think of the last time you were in your house at night and you heard a strange noise; the very possibility that there is someone in your home who should not be there heightens every sense – you hear every tiny sound, your eyes quickly begin to roam around the room.

In Genesis 28 we read the story of Jacob. Fearing for his life (he had pulled a fast one on his brother Esau once too often), he was beginning a long journey to some distant relatives. As Jacob lay down in a field, he had a powerful dream. The Lord showed Jacob the activity of heaven that was always going on – angels descending and ascending from and to heaven. These are angels on assignment, engaged in heavenly activity upon the earth. When Jacob woke up he said, *"Surely the Lord is in this place, and I was not aware of it!"* (Gen. 28:16). God was there, and Jacob nearly missed it. I think this is another aspect of expectation: when we truly are expecting God to break in, we become so alert to every signal that we quickly recognize the activity of heaven in our midst. Without expectation, we miss much of what God is doing or even desires to do. Jesus said to His friends, *"Lift up your eyes and see"* (John 4:35 ESV) – get a new perspective, a new awareness that draws you into participating in heaven's activity. This is part of our lifelong journey: learning to see at a higher plane, to recognize when heaven breaks into our midst.

• • •

In 2004, my wife and I took a team to Kyrgyzstan, a Muslim country that used to be part of the former Soviet Union. We were not allowed to preach on the streets, but people were not hindered from attending meetings that we held indoors. From the first evening, a great deal of healing broke out. And as has always happened throughout history, when the Lord is healing, crowds gather. Over the four evenings, many Muslims came to Jesus. We never once compared Islam and Christianity, or the Koran and the Bible. We simply let them experience the compassionate healing power of Jesus. When they or their loved ones were healed, we would explain that Jesus had another gift for them – a gift that they would always gratefully receive.

During the final evening, a word of knowledge was given that the Lord was about to heal a particular leg condition. I expected about a dozen people to come forward in response; to my amazement, sixty-five came forward. As our team went to them and began to pray for healing, suddenly I was aware that heaven had broken into the room. The only way I can describe it is like a curtain rippling. And the curtain between heaven and that meeting hall in Bishkek suddenly rippled. I simply knew that the power of heaven was there. I called out to the team: "Quickly, pray quickly." There was a great anticipation and urgency inside me. The team looked at me and tried to pray somewhat quicker. But there was a *"suddenly"* about what God was doing. So uncharacteristically (remember, I am a nice quiet Canadian), I hurried to the far side of the platform and began to touch each one of the sixty-five people, running across the platform as I went. And as quickly as I touched them, *every one of them was healed.* Now, I would love to tell you that I always operate in that kind of anointing, but if I did, I would have to repent for lying. So what happened? Heaven suddenly broke in and I managed to recognize it and to respond to what I saw. I was participating in the activity of heaven.

A while ago, Christina and I were talking with a group of young adults in our living room about coming to the nations with us. One young woman said that she could not come until she had her own healing testimony. I asked her what she meant. She replied, "Didn't you know that I've been totally blind in my left eye for twenty years? The optic nerve is dead." I had the young people gather round her and begin to pray. After a minute or two, it happened again – it was like I saw the curtain between the room and heaven ripple. With that came a sudden, strong anointing and a clear sense of specifically how to pray. There was a whole new urgency and authority. Soon, Claire could see light, then she shouted, "I can see your lips moving!" The next day, Claire called to say that she was watching television with her "new eye." By the way, for years Claire had been a patient of the top ophthalmologist in our province, a man who told Claire that he was not a believer, yet pronounced her healing as an unexplainable miracle.

God wants us to lift up our eyes and see from heaven's perspective, which after all is the most real perspective. Over the past few years, as I have sought to encourage people to step into their inheritance to heal the sick in Jesus' name, there is another aspect of this heavenly participation that has been developing. I encourage people to ask the Lord what He is going to do that day, or to show us His activity in an upcoming situation. I am sharing this from a "baby steps" perspective, but along with others on our team, I am beginning to grow in this expression of heavenly anticipation. Before I do outdoor healing and evangelism meetings, I always ask the Lord to show me what He is going to do. I think this pleases Him. The Lord wants His kids to be really connected with what He is doing, and to join Him in it. After all, I was always delighted when my kids came along with me to take part in ministry. It must please Him, because He often shows me hours (sometimes days) before what He is going to do. I do not mean *all* of what He is going to do. God is too wild, too full of surprises for that. (As C.S. Lewis wrote about Aslan, "He's not a tame lion.") But He seems to like to increase our anticipation and sensitivity by showing us *some* of what He is about to do. For years, He has shown Himself to me laughing and joyful. I see my heavenly Father take me by the hand and begin to run. And He says to me, "Come on! Let's go together!" With that, we are running across plowed fields. When

Papa shows me something He is about to do, it is like He is saying, "Let's go together!" There is no greater joy than in being a part of what He is doing. It is what I was made for. It is what every one of His kids was made for, too.

Earlier, I wrote about how a great door for the gospel opened when we were invited into a refugee camp in eastern Kenya, near the Somali border. Most of the one hundred and thirty six thousand had been there for fourteen years. The camp was ninety-seven percent Muslim, but some of the Christians had received permission for our team to come in. For four days we taught them about healing. In the late afternoons, we were permitted to hold outdoor healing evangelism meetings at the edge of the camp – the first ever allowed. Each afternoon, the people gathered in the forty-three degree heat (105 F).

Early one morning as our team gathered to pray, I encouraged each one to ask the Lord to show something He would do at the afternoon meeting. He clearly showed me a man – I saw what he looked like and even the blue shirt he would be wearing. The Lord told me that he was dying of lung disease, but that he was going to be healed. Hours later, as we invited people to come forward for healing, I looked without success for the man. In the midst of the heat and the clouds of dust, there were many hundreds receiving prayer. I climbed back up on the platform (a pile of rice bags) and looked for him – and there he was standing at the back, exactly as I had seen him in the morning, complete with blue shirt. Working my way through the crowd and approached him. I said, "You have a lung disease, don't you?" Surprised, he replied, "Yes, I have had TB for almost seven years, but how do you know that?" I told him what the Lord had shown me. He received this word of knowledge as a personal affirmation from Jesus that He was about to heal him. And that is exactly what happened. His color and countenance suddenly changed; he began to take deep breaths and shouted, "I'm healed." He then told me that for three years, he had been coughing so continuously that he had been unable to sleep for more than two or three hours. Joyously, he testified to what Jesus had done. In fact, for each of the next three days, he asked to testify of his continued healing.

When the Lord shows us what He is going to do, we pray with a whole new level of precision and faith, confident in the result that we are about to see. I am convinced that this is part of our inheritance – to see into the activity of the Kingdom even before it is released. Living our lives with an increased awareness of the possibility of heaven's activity breaking in at any moment, and *expecting* God to do so, changes the way we interact with the world around us. It is what keeps us ready *"in season and out"* (2 Tim. 4:2) – alert to what the Lord's Spirit is doing and to His invitation to participate.

Let us look at some other keys to unlock increased Kingdom activity in our lives.

7

MORE KEYS TO HEALING

He called his twelve disciples to him and gave them authority to drive out evil spirits and to heal every disease and sickness.   MATTHEW 10:1

AUTHORITY

The issue of knowing our authority to heal is of enormous significance. It may be the single biggest factor behind the great increase in healing that we have experienced over the past several years. Authority leads to positive results. Jesus gave His friends authority to do the works of the Kingdom. They went out, ministering in that authority, and what was the result? *"They set out and went from village to village, preaching the gospel and healing people everywhere"* (Luke 9:6).

The disciples were on their first unaccompanied field trip. Until now, they had been watching Jesus do Kingdom works. I am sure that Jesus, as all good teachers would, took them through a process before sending them out. First they observed Jesus. Afterwards, He would have asked them what they noticed – "Did you see what I did with that deaf man before I prayed? I asked the Father, and that is what He told me to do. Did you notice how I took that blind man out of the town? It was because I needed to remove him from the atmosphere of doubt and skepticism that was there" (see Matt. 11:21; Mark 8:23). It was through these kinds of exchanges that they were learning how to release Kingdom activity. Soon, Jesus would have had them try healing the sick and casting out demons with Him watching and coaching, bringing adjustments and encouragement along the way. And in the process, they would have grown in confidence and effectiveness.

The New Testament word for authority is *exousia*, which means the right to exercise power. Not only did Jesus give them the power to release the works of the Kingdom, but He was also saying to them, "This power is yours to use for the Father's purpose; I am entitling you to use Kingdom power, and therefore no one can take that away. They may try to confuse or discourage you by questioning your authority, but their protests are groundless. You have authority to be about the Family Business."

You cannot give away what you do not have, but when it comes to authority, no one has ever had authority like Jesus did, does and always will have. The Father gave all authority to His Son. At the end of Matthew, when Jesus commissioned us to go and make disciples of all nations, He did so out of His place of ultimate authority – *"All authority in heaven and on earth has been given to Me"* (Matt. 28:18). All authority. Nothing lacking.

In Philippians 2, Paul quotes one of the earliest Christian hymns that describes how Jesus emptied Himself (what theologians call the *kenosis*) and how the Father gave Him all authority:

> *God raised him up to the heights of heaven and gave him*
> *a name that is above every other name, so that at the name*
> *of Jesus every knee will bow, in heaven and on earth and*
> *under the earth, and every tongue will confess that Jesus*
> *Christ is Lord, to the glory of God the Father.*
> (Phil 2:9–11 NLT)

The Father gave Jesus a name that proclaimed His authority, a name and authority like no other. That's why Luke said: *"Salvation is found in no one else, for there is no other name under heaven given to men by which we must be saved"* (Acts 4:12). The word used by Luke for saved, *sozo*, is power-packed with meaning: salvation, healing, deliverance, preservation, wholeness. That is the authority that Jesus was given by the Father.

What Jesus had been given, He passed on to His friends, delegating to them the same authority that He had received from the Father. It was time for Kingdom activity to multiply. There was only one way for the disciples to really know that they did, in fact, have authority and that it was effective – they had to test it out. They had to put it into practice. This is what made them powerful. This is what made them dangerous to the enemy. We only truly know what we put into practice. Everything else is just theory. Nothing is more exciting than watching men, women and children bridging the gap between concepts and actualization.

From the time of their commissioning in Matthew 10, the disciples were engaged in a lifestyle of stepping into the activity of the Kingdom. As they did this, they grew in their understanding of the authority that was theirs. In Mark 4:25, Jesus said, *"Whoever has will be given more; whoever does not have, even what he has will be taken from him."* In other words, when it comes to authority, use it and watch it increase, or stay in the realm of the theoretical and watch even what you think you have disappear. Three years of watching and doing meant that Peter grew in his experience of walking in the authority that he really had. When a lame beggar asked him for money, Peter said, *"I don't have any money to give you, but I've got something else – authority. Now get up and walk"* (Acts 3:6 paraphrase) When taken to the house of a church member who had died several hours earlier, Peter exercised his authority and commanded her to rise, which she immediately did (Acts 9:40–41).

From the time that Jesus delegated His authority to him, Peter's journey was not an unbroken trail of success. Peter grew through the many challenges, victories and failures that he experienced. He just kept going. In this issue of healing, of releasing the reality and activity of heaven all around us, the great dividing line is this: in the midst of times of confusion and defeat, will we keep going? I believe that more than anything else, it is the pain of defeat that keeps the church from pursuing our mandate to walk in the authority that Jesus has given us. Healing is a journey marked with both joy and pain – it is clearly not moving from triumph to triumph.

Earlier, I recounted a story about heaven breaking into a meeting in Kyrgyzstan where so many Muslims were healed and saved. But while that was happening, my father died on the other side of the world. I had repeatedly prayed for him, as did a healing prayer team from a nearby city. I couldn't help but ask the Lord, "Why did You move through me to heal so many people that I didn't even know, yet my Dad died?" I do not really have an answer. I know my father is with the Lord. I know God is always good. And I know that I really, really miss my father and wish that, as I have seen with thousands of others, I could have seen him healed. In many ways, the healing journey is a mysterious one. Recently, I heard of a church that decided not to go ahead with healing meetings (before even beginning them) because people might not get healed. The Kingdom is forcefully advancing and it is the forceful who take hold of it. We use our authority, or we lose it.

Healing is a great adventure, and all great adventures involve challenges and difficulties. But adventure carries its own reward. One day the Lord will ask us, "What did you do with the authority I gave you?" As the stories of the minas and the talents clearly show, for those who invested what they were given for the sake of the Father's purposes, there will be great eternal reward, reflecting His pleasure in our faithfulness.

AUTHORITY AND IDENTITY

Our identity reveals our commission. Who we are establishes what we are called to do. What is our primary identity? *"But to all who believed Him and accepted Him, He gave the right to become children of God"* (John 1:12 NLT). Before and after everything else, we are sons and daughters and He gives authority to sons and daughters. Being a son is not a title, but a relationship.

All significant healthy relationships breed confidence and security. This was Jesus' continuous, daily experience. At His baptism, He heard the Father say, *"You are My beloved Son. With You I am well pleased"* (Mark 1:11, ESV). The deepest needs of His soul were met at that moment. He heard His Father say, "You belong to Me. I love you. I am so proud of You." Belonging creates security; being loved becomes our deepest identity; knowing His pleasure results in a deep confidence.

This relationship with His Father is the foundation from which Jesus ministered. He was able to say from His experience, *"The Father loves the Son"* (John 5:20). This infuriated the religious antagonists, who did not understand that relationship gives sons and daughters the experience of Papa's love, while religion can only hope for it. Moving into a confident expectation that God is going to heal through me is intertwined with the confidence that comes with knowing that I am His son.

When our boys were growing up, we lived on a street with a lot of kids. Every afternoon and evening it was alive with the sounds of baseball and football games, street hockey, hide and seek, and such. Behind the street was a big tobogganing hill that, every cold Ontario winter, attracted kids from all over the neighborhood for hours of races and death-defying stunts. When it was time for our boys to come in for supper, I simply had to open the front door and holler, and at least a hundred and fifty kids would swarm into the house, ready to be fed ... of course not! Rather, I would shout, "Suppertime!" and only four boys would run in – and it was the same four boys every evening. Why? Because they knew the sound of my voice and the relationship and authority that my voice carried.

They were Stewarts, and it was Dad Stewart who was calling.

AUTHORITY AND DOMINION

Closely tied to authority is the issue of dominion. When God created the first man and woman, He gave them an assignment:

> *Then God said, "Let Us make man in Our image, according to Our likeness; let them have dominion over the fish of the sea, over the birds of the air, and over the cattle, over all the earth and over every creeping thing that creeps on the earth."* (Gen. 1:26, NKJV)

Theologians call this the Dominion Mandate. As God's representatives on the earth, Adam and Eve were to rule and reign. But dominion means even more: to prevail against, to tread down, and to have power. Exercising authority was not passive, but deliberate and intentional. This involved not only subduing but also multiplication and fruitfulness. In a sense, God was telling them to continue the creation activity that He had begun. They too, were to be creators, under the authority of the Creator. Healing and miracles are creation.

In 2 Corinthians 5:17 Paul writes, *"If anyone is in Christ, he is a new creation"* – literally, "an original formation." Exercising dominion is about restoring life to the way things *originally* were meant to be. Every healing is about taking back territory from the enemy and restoring it to God's *original* intention. We know that Adam and Eve, through unbelief and disobedience, lost dominion. Jesus came as the second Adam to restore what was lost (Matt. 18:11; Luke 19:10).

Dominion and our identity as sons and daughters are directly linked. God's first question, after Adam and Eve disobeyed Him in Genesis 3:9, was "Where are you?" Now, as the father of four sons, I know that my question would have been something like, "What were you thinking!?!" Or maybe even, "What's the matter with you!?!" But with tears in His voice, the Father asked, "Where are you?." He wasn't looking for information, He was expressing the pain in His heart. Relationship had been broken, and it would not be the same again for thousands of years. Notice the order. First they lost relationship, then, they lost dominion. Again, He gives authority to sons and daughters. If we abide in the vine of intimate relationship with the Lord, we will bear much fruit.

Paul goes on to say in 2 Corinthians 5:20, *"Now then, we are ambassadors for Christ"* (NKJV). While driving by the Canadian embassy in Canberra, Australia, this verse came back to me. I thought about how, although it looked like the embassy was in Australia (and obviously it physically was), legally, if I went through its front gate, I would be stepping onto Canadian soil. The ambassador is sent to affect his surroundings (Australia), but serves the purposes of Canada. Another interesting fact is that the ambassador is subject to the laws of the country that sent him, not the laws where he is stationed. We are ambassadors who represent Christ and His Kingdom, and our citizenship is in heaven (Phil. 3:20). The Bible says that we are in the world, but not of the world. We are on assignment to affect change in our surroundings, rather than being changed by them.

THE AUTHORITY IS IN THE MESSAGE

Several years ago, I discovered something very interesting. The authority is in the message itself. Romans 1:16 tells us that it is the gospel which is the power of God unto salvation. The proclamation and demonstration of the Kingdom of God is so powerful that, like an ambassador delivering a message to a foreign government, the message itself does the work. In Mark 4, Jesus says that the Kingdom is like a farmer who plants the seed, then, simply waits, letting the life that is in the seed do its work. *"All by itself the seed produces grain"* (Mark 4:28). I am so thankful for that phrase, *"all by itself."*

In the early '90's, I had the opportunity to get into Russia a day after Gorbachev dissolved the Soviet Union. (More about that later). This began a great adventure whereby I was going into the country several times a year. At that time there was economic chaos and an incredible spiritual hunger after seventy-four years of harsh oppression against Christians.

The Lord gave our teams and me great favor with the government. In fact, on a couple of trips, they provided me with a translator named Paulina. She was a young woman who was the daughter of one of the top leaders in St. Petersburg. Paulina had been educated in the best Marxist-Leninist schools, and as such was an avowed atheist. She would translate for me as I preached in parks, on streets and in crowded subway stations. Many a time, in the midst of my preaching, Paulina would turn to me and whisper, "But Steve, you know I don't believe that!" I would always reassure her and then, I would tell her to go ahead and translate.

On one of these trips, I went straight from the airport to an auditorium, which was provided and paid for by the government. The assignment comes with favor. There was a sizable team of us, and God was doing a lot of wonderful healing. I sensed the Lord wanted me to go to the back of the auditorium where there were bleachers, so I headed back there with Paulina in tow. We found ourselves standing in front of a middle-aged Russian woman who looked very sick indeed. She told us that she had advanced liver disease and that she had a lot of pain in her stomach. This woman's skin was extremely jaundiced and her stomach was very distended. I was uncomfortable to lay my hands on this woman's stomach, so I turned to Paulina and told her to lay her hand on the woman's stomach and to pray as I directed her. Paulina's response was predictable – "But Steve, you know I don't believe." "Paulina, that's all right. Please do this, as I asked." Very tentatively Paulina stretched out her hand and spoke the words I gave her to translate.

No confidence. No faith. But the authority is in the message itself. Suddenly the sick woman shouted, "Fire! Fire! I'm on fire!" So instantly that I could hardly believe my eyes, her color changed from yellow to a healthy pink and her stomach instantly shrank down. All the pain was gone. The people around us cheered. Paulina, the atheist, was used by God because of the "all by itself" of the Kingdom.

When there is an opportunity to release the Kingdom, it seems that our enemy, "the accuser of the brethren," often tries to tell us that somehow we are not prepared. Maybe we have not had any time with the Lord, or maybe we had a conflict with someone this morning that we have not yet worked out. I am certainly not saying that we can ignore relational issues, or that we do not need to keep close to the Lord. But the enemy can no longer use those things to convince us that we must not pray for someone because we are not spiritually or relationally prepared. It is the gospel itself that is the power of God unto salvation (healing, wholeness, restoration, and so on). We release the Kingdom and it does its work.

AUTHORITY AND THE NAME

No discussion of our authority would be complete without at least a brief look at the authority we have in the name of Jesus. At the name of Jesus, every knee will bow. Through His name we release the purposes of God on the earth. Paul told the Colossian church, *"Whatever you do, whether in word or deed, do it all in the name of the Lord Jesus"* (Col. 3:17). The early church understood that God had given us the name of Jesus and all the authority inherent in that name, for our benefit and for the advancement of His Kingdom upon the earth. In the New Testament we read that the early church took Paul's word to heart; in His name the sick were healed and the demonized were set free; they worshiped in the name, their prayers were addressed in the name, they baptized in the name

– all the work of the early church was done in the name of Jesus. This was no tag-on phrase at the end of giving thanks for a meal. They understood the incredible authority that His name carries.

> *The truth is, you can go directly to the Father and ask him, and he will grant your request because you use my name. You haven't done this before. Ask, using my name, and you will receive, and you will have abundant joy* (John 16:23–24 NLT)

Using the name of Jesus is like being given power of attorney; all the power, riches and benefits of Jesus are invested in His name. When we pray, "Father, I ask this in Jesus' name," we are declaring before all spiritual powers that Jesus gave us authority to carry out the Father's will on earth. Jesus endorses our prayer; our request passes out of our hands and into His.

Paul wrote, *"We use God's mighty weapons to pull down the devil's strongholds"* (2 Cor. 10:4 NLT). Jesus' name is our greatest weapon. As my wife and I have learned to use His name with more understanding of the authority it contains, we have seen a wonderful increase in healing and deliverance.

IMPARTATION:
THE KEY TO MULTIPLICATION

One day while I was waiting in an airport on my way home to Canada, I began to daydream about the possibility of going to every village in India just one time. This idea came from my love of Indian villages, especially those that have never heard about Jesus. As I sat there, I pulled out my calculator ... 600,000 villages. That's a lot. What if I could visit ten of them every single day and not stop? What an adventure! I could give myself to that. Now, how long would it take? No. That can't be right – one hundred sixty four years!

Anyone in ministry is faced with the challenge of too much to do, too many places to be, and too little available time. For about three years, Jesus ministered in an area about seventy by forty miles. Yet he commissioned his disciples, and by extension the early church, to take the gospel to the whole world. Quickly, Peter, Paul and the others were faced with the enormity of the task. We are aware of their teaching about raising up disciples, teaching and modeling what it means to follow Jesus. But there is something else that they discovered: they discovered the power of *impartation.*

Randy Clark's book, *There is More!* is an excellent and full examination of this subject that I highly recommend. However, as we look at some key principles for healing, at least a brief consideration of impartation is important.

In Paul's letter to the Romans, he wrote: *"I long to see you so that I may impart to you some spiritual gift to make you strong – that is, that you and I may be mutually encouraged by each other's faith"* (Rom. 1:11–12). It is interesting that Paul, perhaps the greatest teacher in the history of the church, did not say that he longed to come and teach them, but to *impart* to them. Paul knew the power of impartation to change lives and to multiply what the Holy Spirit is doing on the earth. Simply put, impartation is the transfer of anointing from one person to many others. It is not just about training (which is very important); it is about a supernatural acceleration and augmentation of spiritual gifts that the Holy Spirit has given. This is why, as part of every training I do in the various nations, I always include a time of impartation.

The Lord seems to give grace to individuals to impart to others out of their place of primary gifting. So someone who operates in faith and anointing in healing can lay hands on others to receive that healing anointing too. Over the past decade I have had opportunity to pray prayers of impartation over several thousand people. What is exciting about that is the large number of testimonies I have received from many of these people about how they have begun to be used in a greater way to heal the sick themselves.

In the Bible, we see many examples where prayer is accompanied by the laying on of hands, a practice which seems to have had several purposes. Paul reminds the young leader, Timothy, of his commissioning: *"Do not neglect your gift, which was given you through a prophetic message when the body of elders laid their hands on you"* (1 Tim. 4:14). Paul was likely referring to Timothy's ordination. Likewise, Paul and Barnabas had been ordained in Antioch: *"They placed their hands on them and sent them off"* (Acts 13:3). In the gospels, we see Jesus healing and blessing through laying his hands on people. *"And He took the children in His arms, put his hands on them and blessed them"* (Mark 10:16). *"My little daughter is dying. Please come and put your hands on her so that she will be healed and live"* (Mark 5:23). There are many examples of transfer of anointing happening through the laying on of hands in the life of the early church. In Samaria: *"Then Peter and John laid their hands on them and they received the Holy Spirit"* (Acts 8:17). In Ephesus: *"When Paul placed his hands on them, the Holy Spirit came on them, and they spoke in tongues and prophesied"* (Acts 19:6).

As a result of receiving impartation prayer, there has been a great increase in healing when I pray. I have also seen this anointing for healing multiply in others in the Western church and the developing world. Wherever we teach on healing, we follow it with two things: a time of impartation and the injunction to adhere to what Jesus said; namely, *"Freely you have received, freely give"* (Matt. 10:8). This practice moves people beyond just getting more information to empowering and transformation. So the Kingdom advances forcefully – more forcefully than it ever could if I continued in the old model of the "man of God" doing all the ministry. The multiplication of anointing through impartation is one of the most important keys to seeing churches and even communities transformed. It is also a key to making Habakkuk 2:14 tangible: *"For the earth will be filled with the knowledge of the glory of the LORD, as the waters cover the sea."* Men and women, empowered and anointed by the Holy Spirit, release the power of heaven into a desperately needy world.

Impartation is not a one-time event; God desires to come again and again. This is why Paul told the Ephesians, *"Be being filled"* (Eph. 5:18 literal translation). As we embrace a lifestyle of both receiving and releasing, we continue to grow in anointing. Whenever I have met men or women who are moving in anointing, I ask them to pray for me. This has been something that I have been doing for more than twenty years. Likewise, I continue to have the joy of watching others take great strides forward through the power of impartation. It is for all who are hungry, for all who thirst for more of God's presence in their lives. This is the invitation of Isaiah 55:1: *"Come, all you who are thirsty, come to the waters; and you who have no money* [who recognize your need for more than you have], *come, buy and eat!"* God gives to the desperate. And when the anointing comes, it is to be used. Impartation is not an experience. The anointing is an equipping for the work of the Kingdom of God. And as we use it, it grows.

The anointing is not just for the mature; it is for any who are willing to pour out their lives, risking their dignity and security for the sake of the sick and the broken. Several years ago while ministering in northern India, I preached for two nights in a large tent. On the first evening, after inviting men and women to come forward to receive the Lord, I asked the local pastors to come off the platform and help me pray for these new believers. None of them moved. I asked again – still no response. So I went down with my team and we laid hands on each of about seventy-five new believers; many were healed; many had powerful encounters with the Holy Spirit. On the next evening, I invited the sick to come forward and asked the local pastors to come and help me to pray for them. Again, no one moved. I had a large crowd of people who had come forward for healing, so I invited the ones who had come to Christ on the previous night to come forward and help me pray for the sick. The pastors looked uncomfortable, but still did not come help. One of the men who came forward was obviously from the lowest caste; in fact, he looked like a street person. As people lined up to get prayer, no one would receive from this man. Finally someone did and was instantly and powerfully healed. As soon as the crowd realized what had happened, many crowded around this ragged looking man. They too were healed. He was willing to risk; the pastors were not. As a one-day old Christian, he obviously had no maturity. But he *did* have the same Spirit of Christ in him as I or any other believer. To the one who has, even more shall be given. Jesus went on to say, *"To the one who does not have, even what he has will be taken away"* (Mark 4:25). The anointing is to be used. When it is, the Kingdom advances through multiplication.

THE DELIGHT OF GOD

And we can be confident that he will listen to us whenever we ask him for anything in line with his will (1 John 5:14 NLT).

One day, Jesus was in the middle of a Galilean town, busy with the Father's business – healing the sick, setting people free from whatever held them. And of course, wherever Jesus was doing the work of His Father, crowds gathered. Standing back from this boisterous collection of excited people stood a solitary figure. According to Luke the physician, this man was "covered with leprosy," which explains why he stood apart. In those days, leprosy was such a feared disease that, according to Jewish law, anyone suffering from it was responsible to not let anyone get close to them – no matter what, not ever. If anyone did begin to come close, the leper was obliged to shout out, "Unclean! Unclean!" So this man was not only suffering physically, but imagine the deep emotional and social pain that he endured every day of his existence. Now, as he looked over at this healer, Jesus, his desperation overrode the fear and rejection that for years had been stamped upon his soul: *"When he saw Jesus, he fell with his face to the ground and begged Him, 'Lord, if you are willing, you can make me clean'"* (Luke 5:12).

The enemy's relentless assault upon his life had taught this poor man the lesson that he was unworthy and so his only posture was to beg, hoping that somehow Jesus would be willing to extend mercy to him.

What Jesus said to this leprous man is so important for us to understand. Jesus said, *"I am willing"* (Luke 5:13). The New Testament word is *thelo*. New Testament Greek is often much richer in meaning that the English equivalent, and *thelo* is no exception. Its meaning includes volition, but more than that, it means to take pleasure in, to desire, and even to love. Jesus was not saying, "Oh all right, I suppose I'll heal you." He was really saying to this poor, broken man: "Of course, I'll heal you. Are you kidding? I love to heal. It is my great delight and pleasure." By inference, Jesus was sending this man a clear message that he did not have to beg in order for Jesus to heal him. In fact, it was Jesus' delight to heal him.

To be honest, many years of helping and encouraging Christians in the area of healing has shown me that many of them think they have to beg God, or at least talk Him into healing. I hear it in their well-intentioned prayers: "Oh Lord, please heal Mary. She loves you so much. She has really suffered with this pain. Please show her how much you love her and reach down to heal her. And God, it would be such a great testimony to Mary's friends. Please, please, please Lord." This kind of prayer, though heartfelt, is based on a very wrong idea, that we should beg God for healing. God loves to heal. It is His delight, so we never have to beg Him or even try to get Him to agree with the idea. This is a fundamental shift for many of us. When I first realized this, I began to listen to the kind of words that came out of my mouth when I prayed for the sick. Without realizing it, for years I prayed from a "beggar's paradigm." Now that I understand that He delights to heal, I step into healing opportunities with a new confidence and enjoyment.

For me, this issue of God's delight in healing is one of the most significant discoveries that I have ever made. I had understood the issue of *"thelo"* (Mark 1:41) for some time but it was solidified through a powerful experience while Christina and I were conducting a healing conference for some Presbyterian churches in Korea. We had watched the Lord do a lot of healing for three days and it was near the end of the conference. By now almost all the attendees were praying effectively for the sick among them. In the midst of all the healing that was going on a woman brought her twenty-year-old son to me and asked me to pray. The young man explained to me that shortly after birth he had been diagnosed with rheumatoid arthritis and was living with great pain. He rolled up his pants to show me his greatly inflamed and enlarged knees. He explained that he had no memory of ever living without pain. I quietly knelt down in the midst of all the healing activity going on around me, gently placed my hands on his knees, and commanded the rheumatoid arthritis to leave his body in the name of Jesus. He began to feel heat and I began to feel movement happening in his knees under my hands. It was at this point that for me it was as if the room went quiet (In fact, there was a lot of noise going on all around me). I sensed the presence of the Father come very close to me and in my heart I heard Him say, "Son, you really love this, don't you?" I replied, "Yes, Papa, I do." At that moment He said something to me that I think I will never forget; He said simply, "Me too." At this point the young man told me that all the pain had left. He began to walk, run and then, jump off the platform, to his mother's amazement. More than healing, the Kingdom had come to this young man and entirely changed the possibilities for his future. A life rescued.

Hearing these words from my Father has marked me in a deep way. Not only am I completely confident that God delights to heal, I now know that when I pray for the sick, I enter into His delight. I am reminded of a scene in "Chariots of Fire," a movie about Eric Liddell, a missionary who was also an Olympic runner who won the gold medal in 1924. He said this: "God made me to run fast. And when I run, I feel His pleasure." As His children and as His ambassadors, we are given the great privilege of releasing the reality of the Kingdom of God here on earth. When I pray for the sick I feel my Father's pleasure because He simply loves to heal; He *is* healing (Exod. 15:26). But there is another dimension to feeling His pleasure. As any parent knows, it brings joy to see our children engaged in the "sweet spot" of their gifting. To watch a musical child enjoying himself at the piano, or an athletic child excelling in sports brings great satisfaction to their parents. Likewise, when we lay hands on the sick and they are healed, we are operating in the calling and inheritance that we have as His children – and as we do this, He smiles.

Because of the authority that God has given to every disciple of Jesus, and because of His great delight to heal, we can approach the sick and the injured with confidence that the power and momentum of heaven are with us.

Years ago, I heard about a man who was doing amazing work with the poor in his city in the USA. At that time we were in the early stages of planting a church in Canada that we wanted to be marked by compassion for the poor; however, we were unsure of how to really do this effectively. So I arranged to go to spend a couple of days with Steve Sjogren in Cincinnati. I saw his church working with great effectiveness and passion, but frankly, I did not seem to gather any really helpful "tricks of the trade." I still remember flying home and saying to myself, "That's *it*?" Then suddenly the light went on – *"That's* it!" Doing the Kingdom is really quite straightforward. There is very little that is difficult or tricky about it. Just do it. That little revelation all those years ago is one of the most important things that I ever learned. So, just step out and do it.

Having said that, I know that some simple guidelines on *how* to just step out and do it may be helpful. So turn the page. And get ready to step into the activity of the Kingdom.

8

PUTTING HEALING INTO PRACTICE

"Freely you have received, freely give." MATTHEW 10:8

As part of the ministry of Impact Nations, every two or three months we take another group of people from around the Western world to minister in the developing world. Most of the people who come on their first "journey of compassion" have never prayed for the sick before and so, understandably, they approach this with some level of apprehension. Before going out to minister in the villages, we spend the first two days in orientation. An important part of that process is teaching them some practical guidelines for effectively praying for the sick. What I share with them has come out of many years of my own personal experience as well is what I have learned from those who taught me.

In the 1980's John Wimber had a very significant impact upon the church; his teaching and message bridged denominational barriers around the world. John made healing accessible for us all. He presented his now famous "five-step healing model" which impacted countless lives. As I wrote earlier, Bob Brasset is the other major influence for me in the area of healing. From these men I learned both principles and practical advice for effectively praying for the sick.

Here are some of the most important things that I learned, and have tried to pass on to others:

Find out as precisely as possible what the person's problem is. Ask questions like, "Where does it hurt? What do you need? What would you like Jesus to do for you?" Encourage them to be very specific in their answer so that you know precisely for what you are praying. Avoid long lists of conditions; instead tell the person that you will pray for one or two things at a time.

While the person is talking, silently ask God if there is anything else He wants to tell you. Sometimes He will prompt us to ask a particular question: "How long have you had this condition? Is there any other one in your family who has this? Did something traumatic happen to you at around the time when this condition began?" Ask the Lord how He wants you to pray for this person. Because I know that He has given the authority and because I know that He delights to heal, my usual starting point in healing prayer is to command the condition to go. Nevertheless, *I always ask the Lord first* because sometimes He tells me to ask in this situation rather than command.

Before praying, we ask if we can put our hand on the afflicted area. There are many examples of Jesus and the disciples laying hands on the sick. I believe that God uses this in a mysterious but powerful way and I find that the sick never hesitate to say yes. When praying, ask for something specific to happen. Always pray in the name of Jesus; His name is our great weapon. As we pray, check with the person to see what is happening and thank God for whatever He is doing. Thanksgiving is very powerful in healing.

One of the biggest shifts for people in praying for the sick is learning to pray short prayers. With few exceptions I find that we pray much too long, too repetitively, and often too generally. We need to learn to speak specifically to the condition and command it to be healed. In every example we have of Jesus or the disciples healing the sick, they use very few words. I also encourage people to pray with their eyes open. This is for two reasons (besides the fact that after many years of study I have discovered that I can see better with my eyes open than when they are closed!): I want to see the Holy Spirit resting on the person I am praying for. When The Holy Spirit comes, people's bodies usually respond: their eyelids may flutter, they may become flushed; sometimes there is a gentle trembling or some different reaction. When I see something like this then I know that God has shown up, that the *"power of the Lord is here to heal"* (Luke 5:17)

As soon as I have finished praying my short prayer, I ask the person to immediately test it out. With some illnesses this is difficult to do on the spot. So I encourage them to go to a doctor and have themselves checked. But with pain I have them do something they could not do before; for example: moving their arm, bending over or walking around. I always love the look of surprise, almost confusion on people's faces as pain that they have often carried for months or years is instantly gone. If they report that some of the pain is gone but not all of it I tell them, "That is great!", and encourage them that this means God is moving right now and so we will pray again. I do not pray any longer; I simply thank the Lord for what He is doing, command all of the pain to now leave in the name of Jesus, and tell them to check it out again. Almost always all of the pain leaves.

It is at this point that I find out if they have ever invited Jesus into their lives. I do not do this beforehand because of the principle of Mark 1:15 that the Kingdom of God is here for everyone. If indeed they have never invited Christ into their lives, I tell them that the healing that they just received is a gift from Jesus and that He has another gift for them. Then I share very simply the gift of salvation. They have just experienced Jesus on the outside, would they like Him on the inside? The cornerstone of the Gospel is to demonstrate the powerful love of God. When people experience the reality of the Kingdom, their hearts are powerfully and immediately drawn to the King. Through experiencing the healing power of God and His Kingdom we have seen thousands upon thousands of people come joyfully to Jesus Christ – Muslims, Buddhists, Hindus, and people in the shops and on the streets of our own towns and cities.

In order to make what I have written as simple and extensible as possible, I will finish by including Bob Brasset's healing prayer guidelines:

FIVE SIMPLE HEALING STEPS

Ask What's Wrong

First, we ask the person what the need is, or what they would like Jesus to do. Even Jesus asked the blind man: "What do you want?" It is a step of faith for the person. This can happen in any setting, a shopping centre for instance. If we hear a need we just say: "May I pray for you?"

Listen to God

Next, we listen for wisdom from the Holy Spirit. Sometimes He directs us to ask further questions about how the condition developed. Was it an accident? Is it in the family and inherited? Sometimes we have a revelation, but usually we just move on.

Invite God's Presence

Thirdly, we ask very simply: "Lord, pour Your love on this person." Pray with your eyes open and watch. It's amazing what happens when God's love begins to come on the person. Sometimes people begin to reel to and fro as God's love saturates them, or they feel heat, or peace. Sometimes they don't sense it, but we do. Whatever the response, the attention is on God and His love for the person, not on the problem. God totally loves them, and has great grace and favor for them.

Command the Healing

In the simplest way, we command the affliction to go and the body to be healed. We speak to the condition rather than praying for God to heal it. Pray a very short prayer. "Joint pain go, and elbow be healed in Jesus' name!" The faith command is important. Just this one change of approach from asking to commanding will increase miracles. We are doing what Jesus told us to do, rather than praying for God to do it. This is the way Jesus and the disciples ministered healing.

It seems that in the presence of the 'love anointing,' which is really God Himself (God is love), there is great authority for these 'love commands.' After all, healing is an expression of God's love.

Test It Out

Finally, after the shortest time (10-20 seconds), we ask the person to test themselves and see what happened. Two things seem to be important here. First, don't stall or hesitate at the healing part, but act quickly in faith. We can sometimes pray our way right out of the anointing. We aren't trying to convince God to heal. He wants to heal. His love is already here and He commissioned us to walk in His love and to heal. We do it. Secondly, it is important that the person quickly do what they could not do as an act of faith. Jesus would say: "Get up and walk!" or "Stretch out your hand!" The moment they notice improvement or complete healing, thank Jesus. If there is improvement, but not yet total healing, simply pray again. Of course, some conditions cannot be tested immediately and so we encourage them to go to their doctor to be checked out.

JOURNAL ENTRY:
THE HIDDEN MANILA

I am trying not to fall down. Cha, Rogel and I are following a woman named Dalia as we wind single-file through a dark labyrinth of shacks set too close for any sun to get in; she is taking us to her aged mother who is too weak and sick to get to the clinic that we have set up in a basketball court. Only fifty yards from the court, I have stepped into another world. After a few twists and turns I am completely disoriented. A very large dog bares its teeth at me and snarls menacingly. In the gloom, I almost trip over a laundry woman crouching beside a large bowl filled with clothes. The alley is so narrow that I have to turn sideways just to pass. Children are everywhere, but they are eerily quiet. I am so intent on not losing my footing that I hit my head on a low hanging metal roof. Another sharp corner and suddenly we are in front of a low door. Dalia invites us in to meet her mother, Lola. The old woman is tribal – she was raised in some distant village in the hills. Like most nations, the Philippines have a First Nations population; and like all nations, they represent the poorest, most disenfranchised in the country. Lola seems to be waiting for us; perhaps her daughter had promised to get help somehow.

Lola can't see, can barely hear and she has constant pain in her hip which is the result of a fall she had escaping the fire that tore through this area two years ago. After prayer she still can't see, but her hearing has cleared up completely (She told us that everything was suddenly too loud!). We have Lola walk and she thinks her hip is better, but without sight, she is reluctant to walk

129

very much. Cha asks Dalia how we can pray for her. She earns a living by washing clothes, but sometimes there are no clothes to wash. When this happens, Dalia and her mother do not eat. As we pray, her tears begin to fall. Cha simply holds Dalia as her pain and fear come out through her weeping. We go back to the clinic to get her some vitamins; this is all they have asked for. Like most of the truly poor, these women expect so little and are so thankful and surprised when any care or attention is given.

"The poor you shall have with you always." This is such a misunderstood scripture. How often I have heard it quoted by church members to justify not giving the poor much attention. How could any thinking person believe that Jesus was excusing us from ignoring the poor because they are always there anyway? Jesus, who *fully identified* with the poor. Jesus, who chose to be born into the servant class, to become a political refugee in Egypt, to be homeless (Luke 9:58). Jesus was giving disciples their identity. True disciples are those who have the poor among them, who see the poor and make room for them in their lives. Jesus said that true disciples must be where He is. And He was with the poor. He still is. I have been reading the Beatitudes over and over again for a few months now – in both Matthew's gospel and Luke's. There is something very disconcerting about Luke 6:20–26. Jesus blesses the poor and warns the rich. As Thomas Merton once wrote, why do I want to get rich when the One I follow chose to be poor? No answers yet, but a fair bit of discomfort.

Today's medical clinic (and Lola's home) are in an area called Addition Hills. It is only two minutes from one of the main roads in Manila, lined with modern office buildings, Starbucks, shopping malls and some very nice looking churches (Earlier, a pastor had taken me through one of them, showing me the new recording studio and the marble floors in the foyer). Two minutes away. Another world.

I spent some time with Rogel today, after our visit to Lola. He and his wife have been working in their spare time in Addition Hills for some time now. It is one of the poorest districts in Manila; there are over one hundred thousand people living in grinding poverty. Children roam the streets because there is no more room at the one public school. So they can't go to school, just like most of their parents. A perfect formula for perpetual poverty. Rogel and some of his friends pool their money to feed as many as they can. Currently they can provide five hundred meals, twice a month. Rogel says that this is the only time they will get meat all month. The cost for one thousand meals is $250 USD. I asked him how many of the Manila churches are working in Addition Hills. He said none. I re-asked the question because obviously we had misunderstood each other. But no. The answer is *none*. Dear Lord Jesus, please forgive us. Awaken Your church. Let us find You where You really are.

9

THE REVOLUTION OF JESUS

"I have come to bring fire on the earth, and how I wish it were already kindled!"   LUKE 12:49

The Kingdom of God brings a revolution, a new order that challenges and changes the status quo. The Gospel was so revolutionary, so threatening to the political, military, economic and religious Powers That Be (and the dark spiritual powers behind them) that they executed Jesus and chased down his disciples. This was not because Jesus cared for the poor or healed the sick; it was because he declared a whole new order. From that time until this, the Powers That Be have done, and continue to do all that they can to domesticate the revolutionary message of Jesus. In large part, this is why such a small gospel is preached in our day.

The Apostle Paul wrote about the spiritual Powers That Be:

For we are not contending against flesh and blood, but against the principalities, against the powers, against the world rulers of this present darkness, against the spiritual hosts of wickedness in the heavenly places (Eph. 6:12 RSV).

He was reminding the Ephesians that they must not limit themselves to natural perceptions, but be aware of supernatural opposition. Yet, in his letter to Titus, Paul writes: *"Be subject to principalities and powers"* (Tit. 3:1 KJV). The New Testament tells us that the

Powers are not just physical, but also spiritual; not one or the other, but both. Many evangelicals see the Powers as being "out there"; however Paul's integrated worldview presented the Powers as being spiritual entities at work in the institutions where they reside.

How do the Powers That Be infiltrate the institutions of society, including businesses, government, economic and social structures, even churches and families? God has created every institution with a redemptive purpose, part of His overall plan to bring all things under Christ. Whenever an institution abandons its God-created purpose for its own self-interest, it moves into a place of idolatry (which is following after anything other than God and His calling). In turn, idolatry always opens the door to the demonic or, as Paul writes, "spiritual hosts of wickedness." This is why Satan works through known institutions and structures to oppose God's cosmic plan of reconciliation and restoration.

Thirty years before Jesus began his ministry, God announced His revolution when He sent an angel to Mary. Her son, Jesus the Messiah, would bring a whole new order. Mary prophesied this new order in Luke 1 in a prophetic proclamation known as the Magnificat.

> *"Oh, how my soul praises the Lord.*
> *How my spirit rejoices in God my Savior!*
> *For he took notice of his lowly servant girl,*
> *and from now on all generations will call me blessed.*
> *For the Mighty One is holy,*
> *and he has done great things for me.*
> *He shows mercy from generation to generation*
> *to all who fear him.*
> *His mighty arm has done tremendous things!*
> *He has scattered the proud and haughty ones.*
> *He has brought down princes from their thrones*
> *and exalted the humble.*
> *He has filled the hungry with good things*

and sent the rich away with empty hands.
He has helped his servant Israel
and remembered to be merciful.
For he made this promise to our ancestors,
    to Abraham and his children forever."
(Luke 1:46–55 NLT)

I do not think it can be overstated how revolutionary this passage is. One of my favorite writers, E. Stanley Jones, called the Magnificat the most revolutionary document in the world. Years ago I was amazed to read that during the British occupation of India, the Archbishop of Canterbury instructed all of his priests in India to never read the Magnificat in public as it was "too seditious," that its powerful message would open the doors to social and political upheaval. This passage is a prelude to all that will follow in Luke's account, which is the most "social" of the four Gospels; in Luke's account we see Jesus very specifically addressing and ministering to the poor.

In Luke's account of the Beatitudes, part of what is known as the Sermon on the Plain, Jesus singles out the truly poor and hungry; He brings hope and comfort to those who weep:

Blessed are you who are poor,
for yours is the kingdom of God.
Blessed are you who are hungry now,
for you shall be satisfied.
Blessed are you who weep now,
for you shall laugh.
(Luke 6:20–21 ESV)

When Matthew records these blessings in the Sermon on the Mount, he presents a more spiritual emphasis on Jesus' words where He says, *"Blessings on the poor in spirit, for theirs is the kingdom of heaven"* and *"Blessings on those who are hungry and thirsting after righteousness, because they will be satisfied"*

(Matt. 5:4, 6 paraphrase). We can mistakenly assume from Luke's account that Jesus is saying that it is wonderful to be poor, to be hungry, to be weeping. However, it is clear that in the Kingdom of God Jesus intends to bless the physically poor and hungry. He made a point of demonstrating this by feeding the five thousand – the only miracle recorded in all four Gospels. In this passage we see Jesus identifying with the poor, being on their side. The gospel poor are the world's marginalized and downtrodden people, the ones without other options. These verses are an invitation to the poor and hungry of the earth to cry out to God in the midst of their poverty, rather than to succumb to hopelessness or bitterness. Jesus is saying, "I'm here with you. I am fully identifying with you. And that Kingdom I have prepared is for *you* in a very special way."

The Magnificat is both a promise to those at the bottom of the social order and a warning to those at the top. *"He has scattered the proud in the imaginations of their hearts. He has put down the mighty from their thrones ... The rich he has sent away empty"* (Luke 1:51–53 NKJV). In God's new order, where up becomes down, no longer is value given according to a person's wealth or status. This is not only counter-cultural; it is counter-intuitive. We live in a world that says, and has always said, that value is based upon performance, wealth and power. James, in one of the earliest letters written to the church, addressed this very issue, challenging the church not to give preferential treatment to the wealthy and influential. James tells the church that showing partiality is sin, plain and simple. This calls for a value adjustment, the value of God's Kingdom. *"Listen my beloved brothers, has not God chosen those who are poor in the world to be rich in faith and heirs of the kingdom?"* (Jam. 2:5 ESV). Martin Luther called the honoring of the successful, "the greatest and most universal belief or religion on earth." When we truly embrace this revolutionary Gospel of the Kingdom, it challenges our motives, causes us to see our failings for what they are, and presses us into the grace of our Savior.

. . .

For a long time, we have heard about "Trickle-down Economics." If the rich become richer, then eventually it will bring a benefit for the middle class and poor. To their own self-interest, the Powers That Be, those political, economic and social structures and powers that seek to maintain the status quo (and thereby resist the truth of God's Kingdom), constantly perpetuate this economic theory which is merely a justification for the rich to continue to acquire more and more. The Magnificat declares how God deals with such greed and selfishness. God confronts the proud, the selfishly powerful and the rich.

Jesus declared and represented God's new order, His Kingdom. To see God's priorities and desires, we need look no further than Jesus and how He lived his life. Jesus did not seek out the rich and the powerful so that His Kingdom could have maximum influence. Instead, He joined those at the bottom, the outcasts and the undesirables. Jesus could have come to earth as the son of anyone He wanted; He could have come as the son of the Emperor Tiberius or a great business leader or esteemed religious leader in Israel. Instead, even in His birth, He identified with the weak and the lowly. Jesus' mother was a member of the servant class. *"For He has regarded the lowly state of His servant"* (Greek: *doulos*). If we have any doubt about Jesus' choice to come to earth as a member of the poor, we need look no further than Luke 2:24. When Joseph and Mary presented Jesus at the Temple, they brought with them *"a pair of turtledoves, or two young pigeons."* According to Leviticus 12:8, a family was to bring a lamb, but if they were too poor, they could bring two turtle doves or pigeons. And of course there was the issue of the circumstances of Jesus birth. In this way he identified with all of those who, from the earliest days of their memory, live with a sense of being somehow unacceptable. Shortly after Jesus' birth, an angel warned Joseph that King Herod was trying to kill Jesus. Joseph escaped to Egypt with his young family and lived there in hiding for two years. Thus Jesus' own life points to his compassion and identification with refugees around the world.

In response to a request from a man who wanted to travel with Jesus, He replied, *"Foxes have dens to live in, and birds have nests, but the Son of Man has no home of his own, not even a place to lay his head"* (Luke 9:58 NLT). Jesus chose homelessness during his years of ministry. In my city there are several thousand homeless men and women. They live in empty lots, on the sidewalks, under the bridges and in alleyways. While Jesus likely did not live in these exact conditions, He did choose to reject the comfort of a home. Perhaps whenever we see the homeless, we should think of Jesus. Over the years I have become convinced that in a very special way His presence is manifested among the poor. That is why I often tell people before we go out to demonstrate God's love among the poor, "Remember, we are not taking Jesus to the poor; He is already there waiting for us."

The Magnificat reveals God's heart and intentions toward the poor and disenfranchised; within it we see the rhythm of God's new order, the Kingdom. It reflects a major theme of the Gospel – God sees and respects the poor, He lifts them up, He fills them up with good things, He feeds the poor, He remembers the poor and He helps them.[6] Scripture reveals God's passion for justice for the poor and the weak, the widow and the orphan, the outcast and the foreigner.

Scripture challenges me, calling me to shift from my values to God's values. That is why for disciples, this revolution is very personal. More than just calling our attention to what needs to change in the social, economic and political systems "out there," Jesus calls us to an interior revolution – a revolution of our values, our priorities, our passions. When we gave our lives to Jesus, something powerful and mystical happened. We were born from

6 Edward F. Markquart, <http://www.sermonsfromseattle.com/series_c_magnificat.htm>.

above (or born again). Living as a Christian is not meant to be something we add on to our lives as some sort of self-fulfillment or self-improvement program. We are called to a whole new life, a life that is directed and empowered by the Spirit of Christ now living in us. Paul says that we have become a whole new creation, part of this new revolutionary order.

A NEW ALLEGIANCE

The single most repeated saying of Jesus in the Gospels is this:

> *If anyone would come after me, he must deny himself and take up his cross and follow me. For whoever wants to save his life will lose it, but whoever loses his life for me will find it* (Matt. 16:24–25).

Jesus spoke these words immediately after telling his disciples that He would soon face suffering and death. Jesus was consciously and actively moving toward the cross. He chose. Jesus knew that His execution was the inevitable result of clashing with both the spiritual and structural Powers That Be. Jesus called His disciples to follow Him in suffering; He knew that they would grow in faith and spiritual power through participating in suffering. Jesus does not call disciples to a life of concepts, principles, or theological theories; discipleship is not an abstract program. This is why I am committed to continuously taking men and women to the front lines of ministry, whether in the West or in the developing world. Jesus trained His disciples through teaching, demonstration and release. Neither the classroom nor the pulpit on their own will lead people into the kind of discipleship that impacts the world.

What does it mean to "take up your cross"? For the disciples the invitation to take up their cross was understood literally since in their day cross-bearing was an all too common and terrifying sight. Today, for many thousands of our brothers and sisters in the developing world this is also a literal invitation to die for the sake of the gospel. "Voice of the Martyrs" reports that about one hundred seventy-five thousand Christians die for their faith annually. This is a five-fold increase over the last hundred years. Through Impact Nations, I work with heroic men and women – disciples – who have lost loved ones, employment and homes for the sake of the Gospel. It is interesting to note that in first century Jerusalem, crucifixion was always public. Really dying to ourselves will mean a turning away from values and worldviews. It cannot be hidden.

But for us in the West whose lives will most likely not be in mortal danger if we follow Jesus, what does it mean to "carry our cross"? Jesus' invitation to carry our cross does not mean to simply tolerate the trials and troubles of life without complaint. A difficult marriage, financial difficulty, career challenges – these are merely the challenges of life that Jesus said we would all experience. To see these as cross-bearing is to minimize the call to true discipleship.

Again, the gospel that Jesus proclaimed was revolutionary; its purpose has always been to call out a new community, counter-cultural in its allegiance to a new Master. By its very nature, this revolutionary gospel positions this new community of disciples in conflict with the values of the world around it. Following Jesus means committing to live counter-culturally, rejecting the world's systems that falsely offer security and significance. Following Him means saying, "Jesus is Lord, and Caesar is not," or "Jesus is Lord, and my retirement plan is not, my national identity is not." Following Him means being a prophetic voice against injustice. It means living a very intentional and purposeful life. If we truly decide to let Another One rule, if this decision is real and sustained, then it *will* change the direction and priorities of our lives. If I obey Jesus' words to share what I have with those who lack, it will directly affect my financial standing. If I leave my family and friends for the sake of the mission field, it will affect relationships, causing me real loss. If I make a stand for non-violence as I seek to follow Jesus in loving my enemies and turning the other cheek when my country is at war, it separates me from other citizens (sometimes even from my own church). If I choose to follow Jesus into a simple life, this separates me from the standards of my community and opens me to great potential for misunderstanding and even contempt.

Jesus anticipated this pressure to conform when he said, *"You are the salt of the earth. But if the salt loses its saltiness, how can it be made salty again? It is no longer good for anything, except to be thrown out and trampled by men"* (Matt. 5:13). In ancient times salt was used primarily for seasoning, health and preservation. Salt was essential to prevent decay. Disciples were to serve as a deterrent to the moral and spiritual decay of the world. Yet there is intense pressure on us not to be too obviously Christian. This may come overtly from co-workers, neighbors and relatives; however, the greater danger lies in the covert and pervasive attack on nonconformity and loyalty to a radically different worldview. Jesus is saying that if we do not consciously and consistently choose to live as disciples, gradually we will lose our distinctiveness. Eventually we will become irrelevant, "trampled by men" – either the object of scorn, or perhaps worse, total disinterest. For a number of years, studies have shown that in North America, there are very few discernible differences in behavior between Christians and non-Christians, including employee theft, truth telling, divorce and even household violence. Surely it is time for the church to move on from a salvation that does not meaningfully progress beyond the altar call. It is time for the church to rediscover and once again proclaim without compromise the radical demands of Jesus Christ.

I am convinced that following Jesus is not the same as being a believer. Christians go to heaven; disciples follow Jesus as they change the world. Simply put, disciples are those who have heard and responded wholeheartedly to the call of Jesus the Revolutionary.

When we recognized our need for a Savior, turned from our sin and embraced the healing and forgiveness of Jesus, we were saved. Yet we are still being saved. This sanctifying work of God's Spirit will continue every day of our lives. This is why we need to be constantly called, as C. S. Lewis wrote, "further up and further in." We are invited to enter into God's rhythm where we begin to see His perspective of the poor, to encourage and feed them, and to find ways to meaningfully help them. Remember that Jesus told us that when we do these things for the poor, we are doing them to Him.

This revolution takes us beyond acts of charity (which are good) to learning what it means to defend the poor, the widow and single mom, orphans and latch-key kids, and the oppressed. There are a growing number of outstanding Christian organizations developing key strategies and tactics coming against forces of injustice in the developing world.

As we have seen in the Magnificat, the Gospel declares a great leveling – "*He has brought down rulers from their thrones but has lifted up the humble. He has filled the hungry with good things but has sent the rich away empty.*" Hundreds of years earlier, Isaiah foresaw the breaking in of the Kingdom of God. He described the proclamation of John the Baptist with these words:

> *A voice of one calling:*
> *"In the desert prepare*
> *the way for the LORD ;*
> *make straight in the wilderness*
> *a highway for our God.*
> *Every valley shall be raised up,*
> *every mountain and hill made low."*
> (Isa. 40:3–4)

When those coming to be baptized asked John how their repentance should be lived out, he told them they should share extra food and clothing with those who have none, and they should live justly and honestly. Throughout His ministry Jesus taught that disciples care for the hurting and the weak and the hungry. This was understood and lived in the early church, encouraged by the apostles. Paul called for sacrificial giving that there might be equality among believers from different countries (2 Cor. 8:13–15). If we are truly going to participate in the Revolution of Jesus, as disciples who will deny ourselves and follow Him where He is going, then surely "losing our lives to find them" must include sacrificial, meaningful giving to our desperately poor family in the developing world

And yet ... *"Whoever loses his life for Me will find it."*

This is an invitation full of promise. Like the man who found the treasure in the field, the joy of the life we have discovered so outweighs the price that, in time, we can hardly remember the cost. This is why Jesus told Peter, *"And everyone who has given up houses or brothers or sisters or father or mother or children or property, for my sake, will receive a hundred times as much in return and will inherit eternal life"* (Matt 19:29 NLT). There is a freedom and an abandonment in this kind of life. Jesus invites us to fully commit, not relying upon the social and financial safety net of the world (which are after all largely illusory), but to follow Him into the great adventure of life as He intended it to be.

For a number of years, I have had the joy of taking men and women into frontline ministry around the developing world and watching them come alive as they discover what God had really put inside them. Recently those were the words I heard from a man who had returned from a Journey of Compassion to Nicaragua. A woman told me that when her husband goes out to the mission field with Impact Nations, he comes alive, and that is because he is living with a greater purpose. I cannot count the number of times that people have said to me upon their return from a Journey where they led people to Christ, were used to heal the sick, the blind and the deaf, and where they brought Good News to the poor through food and medicine – "I am a different person than I thought I was. My life has changed." This is because we were made for the Kingdom. Just as Jesus rescued us, we are invited to be rescuers, active participants in His greater story. As I wrote earlier, we were created with a desire for significance, and the greatest place of significance that we can ever find is in God's plan for the restoration and re-creation of the earth.

Embracing the Kingdom calls for a revolution of values, priorities and allegiances. This is why Jesus said we cannot be part of what He is doing if, after starting out, we longingly look back to what we used to have (Luke 9:62). It takes courage to follow Jesus into His Kingdom with abandonment, but courage is rewarded – both in this life and the next – by the One who holds all things in His hands.

SETTING THE CAPTIVES FREE

In early 2010 while traveling to several nations in Africa, I encountered a remarkable man named Mike Brawan. Mike had been orphaned at eight years of age and lived the next four years in a garbage dump. Following that, he lived on the streets of Nakuru, Kenya. One evening Mike went to a large Crusade. He did not go there because of any spiritual hunger but because, as he told me, "If you can't pick people's pockets when their hands are raised in worship, then you just can't pick pockets." While there, he heard the Gospel, responded, and the entire direction of his life changed. Today Mike oversees about fifty churches, is a city councillor, and has started over fifty small businesses for the poor.

One day Mike told me about an incredible situation going on in the women's prison in Nakuru. When women are arrested for petty crimes such as selling vegetables on the side of the road without a license or making home brew liquor, if they cannot pay the fine, they are put in prison typically for six to twelve months. If they have small children, they are put in the cell with their mother and stay with her for the duration of the sentence. The children are not allowed to leave the cell and many die from bad water, lack of medical care, or malnutrition. When I said that Impact Nations would like to help,

Mike went to the mayor and to the warden of the prison and made arrangements for sixteen women and their children to be released once their fine was paid. We put this need on the Impact Nations website, letting people know that for eighty-eight dollars a woman and her children would be freed, the woman would receive a six-month work permit, and where needed, she would receive job re-training. There was an overwhelming and immediate response on the website. Within days pictures of the women and children along with their stories were sent to us from Kenya. Because of the response, the warden allowed another group of sixteen women and children to have their fines paid and be released. Men and women from all over the world were both encouraged and deeply touched by the heartfelt thanks and stories of these women. Through this very tangible demonstration of the Kingdom of God, Muslim women spontaneously gave their lives to Christ. Several of the stories were bittersweet as we read about women who had a child die in the cell before they were released. One woman wrote that when her one-year-old child died, leaving her with a three-year-old child still living in the cell with her, she came to such a point of despair she began to plot how she could take her own life. It was at this time that Mike came to her cell and amazed her with the announcement, "You're free! Someone on the other side of the world has paid your fine."

This is the rhythm of the King and His Kingdom. When we walk in His rhythm, we walk in a favor that sets captives free.

In his Inaugural Address of Luke 4:18–19, Jesus declared:

> *"The Spirit of the Lord is on me,*
> *because he has anointed me*
> *to preach good news to the poor.*
> *He has sent me to proclaim freedom for the prisoners*
> *and recovery of sight for the blind,*
> *to release the oppressed,*
> *to proclaim the year of the Lord's favor."*
> (Cited from Isaiah 61:1–2)

Jesus was announcing that what Mary had prophesied thirty years earlier, had now begun. Like the Magnificat, these words proclaimed that a whole new order was now coming. For years I embraced the literal healing of the blind and good news to the poor and oppressed, yet assumed that freedom for the prisoners was to be understood as those who are bound up spiritually. The Kingdom is powerful enough to defeat injustice, wherever it happens – even in a federal prison.

The Lord underlined this truth seven months later, this time at the men's prison in Nakuru (He often has to teach me something more than once before I get it). Because of what had happened in freeing the women and children, for the first time ever, Mike was given permission to hold a Christmas meal and celebration for the men in the maximum security prison. As part of their punishment, these men are never allowed to eat meat. Mike and his team killed and roasted eight bulls that day. The men had never seen such a feast! But the Lord was just getting started.

As the men sang and Mike spoke, the Holy Spirit fell upon this huge prison. Mike described it to me like this: "Revival suddenly hit all of us!" In the midst of this move of God, something incredible happened – the prison authorities came to Mike and told him that then and there, they would pardon *two hundred men* and *who* would be pardoned was up to Mike and his team. Among those prisoners who were set free (Luke 4:18) were three men who were awaiting capital punishment and four men who had been in the prison for at least thirty-six years.

There is another part to this Christmas story. One of the freed prisoners is a man named Elly Otieno. When Elly was sixteen, he got into a fight with his friend. Tragically, his friend was killed. Until this amazing Christmas, Elly has spent forty-six years in prison. When Elly got out, he was a forgotten man. Here is what Mike wrote:

"Coming out of prison, Elly could not find any of his family members since it has been a long time for him in prison, hence they

forgot about him. He got saved and is now committed to serve the Lord all his remaining years and he is now with us in the Church."

Mike found some relatives of the friend that had been killed all those years ago, and he took Elly to them for a time of forgiveness and restoration. For a sixty-two-year-old man, God is restoring the years the locusts have eaten. For two hundred men, God has granted a gift of grace and a demonstration of the power and love of a Father that they will never forget. The Father took Elly, a forgotten, lonely man, and placed him in a family, the family that Jesus talked about in Matthew 12.

WHO IS MY FAMILY?

Jesus was teaching in a crowded house:

> *As Jesus was speaking to the crowd, his mother and brothers stood outside, asking to speak to him. Someone told Jesus, "Your mother and your brothers are outside, and they want to speak to you." Jesus asked, "Who is my mother? Who are my brothers?" Then he pointed to his disciples and said, "Look, these are my mother and brothers. Anyone who does the will of my Father in heaven is my brother and sister and mother!"* (Matt. 12:46–50).

Jesus seems to be saying that in following Him, we will discover a whole new meaning of family. And not surprisingly His definition of family is a revolutionary, radical one. Jesus is telling us that in His revolutionary family, something new has been created, something that runs deeper than biology or sociology, or geography, or nationality. This whole new family that is without borders reflects the character of our seeking and inviting God.

During a Journey of Compassion in Andhra Pradesh, India, we heard about a remarkable miracle and went to investigate. The Lord had used a pastor with whom we had been working for some time to raise a four-year-old girl from the dead. She had been dead for a few hours when her family brought her to Santayya to perform the funeral. Instead, he prayed for her and the Lord raised her up. News of this spread rapidly around the area, and since we had worked with Santayya for a couple of years, one of the staff from Impact Nations went up to investigate. Sure enough, they introduced him to the little girl (who was now running around with her friends). While there, Doug was taken to the home of a blacksmith. This poor man earned about a dollar a day, and on this he was supporting his family. When Doug met the family, one member would not look at him. After four years of marriage, Sunitha had recently been cast off by her husband. With no place to go, she returned to her father's home in disgrace. Now she lived with the shame of being a castoff, ineligible for marriage; but more than that, Sunitha lived with the shame of being a financial burden to her father.

My friends asked her father if Sunitha could drive with them the two hours back to our sewing school for women at risk. Without hesitation, her father sent her away with us. Sunitha quickly packed up her few belongings and her small daughter. When we shared her story with the Journey of Compassion team, one member immediately decided to pay for Sunitha's six month training as well as her room and board. Not only did her financial future immediately change (upon graduation, Sunitha would be earning at least five dollars a day), but also she and her daughter were invited into a healthy family setting. Instead of the shame of rejection, they experienced the joy of acceptance; instead of the pain of isolation, they were brought into the security of community.

Once again, Jesus made the Gospel exchange: *"Beauty for ashes, joy for sadness, praise for despair"* (Isa. 61:3).

In Paul's letter to the Galatian church he said,

> For you are all children of God through faith in Christ
> Jesus. And all who have been united with Christ in baptism
> have put on the character of Christ, like putting on new

clothes. There is no longer Jew or Gentile, slave or free, male and female. For you are all one in Christ Jesus (Gal. 3:26–28 NLT).

Jesus had no boundaries in His family and He lived this out. Contrary to the standards and expectations of society at that time, Jesus' family included outcasts, tax gatherers, healed beggars and at least one prostitute.

"*Anyone* who does the will of my father is family" (paraphrase) This is a very challenging indeed. Jesus is telling me that I have family in the dumps in Nicaragua, Kenya and Manila. He is telling me that I have about one million Iraqi family members now under constant threat and danger. And what about my family in Sudan – millions of them who are being killed, raped and sold into slavery? (The current value for one of these brothers is $15,000). And what about my fifty thousand brothers and sisters in Orissa, India, whose homes were burned down and as they sought to escape, many of them were murdered along the road?

Like most of you, I pray for my children and grandchildren, my close friends and those around me with particular needs. But the revolution that Jesus declares presents me with a whole new set of family values. I have family members who are homeless, who are starving, who are struggling with AIDS and who are suffering countless forms of oppression.

Martin Luther King once said that we are *"bound by allegiances and loyalties which are broader and deeper than nationalism... This call for a worldwide fellowship that lifts neighborly concern beyond one's tribe, race, class and nation is in reality a call for an all-embracing and unconditional love for all"*[7]

• • •

---

7 Martin Luther King Jr., *A Time to Break Silence, A Testament of Hope* (New York: HarperCollins, 1986), 242.

We live in a time where ideas hold more interest than action. My challenge is to not settle for theory, principles and ideas but to take the truth of the Gospel and apply it – no matter how painfully – to my daily living. The way I live my life reveals what I *really* believe about God and His kingdom. If it is true that revolutions change *everything*, then I must continue to ask myself, "Am I letting God's revolution change me? And where does it still need to change me?"

Sometimes these questions can make me feel overwhelmed and I find my heart shutting down. Recently, a Canadian man was with me for a day in a poor barrio in Central America. After watching our Impact Nations team conducting a medical clinic, doing repairs at a school and praying for the sick on the streets and in their homes, he said to me, "Don't you feel like you're trying to empty the ocean with a teacup?" It is funny, but that thought had never occurred to me. I told him that we are simply caring for the ones that God has put in front of us today. As Heidi Baker has famously said, we must learn to "Stop for the one." This is how we move in the rhythm of the Kingdom. Compassion is about the next person ... and then the next. And when I start to feel overwhelmed and stressed, discouraged and tired, I remember once again that Jesus' heart really is big enough for every person in every village and every town and every nation.

10

GOD'S RESTORATION:
THE KINGDOM AND JUSTICE

Let justice roll on like a river, righteousness like a never-failing stream.   AMOS 5:24

The issue of justice is central in the heart of God. There are over two thousand scriptures about justice in the Bible. In Genesis, Abraham begins to discover that this God that he has encountered is personally engaged in issues of justice, provoking Abraham to intercede on behalf of Sodom. Moses is presented with a Law for corporate living that is founded on God's passionate insistence that the emerging nation of Israel live justly. Through the historical and prophetic books of the Old Testament we see the Lord interacting with Israel as they either pursue or ignore His demands for justice. Jesus began His ministry declaring justice: freedom for the prisoners and release for the oppressed (Luke 4:18). He proclaimed justice to the nations and caused justice to be victorious (Matt. 12:18-20 NLT). The Apostle Peter tells the church that their faith was given to them *"because of the justice and fairness of Jesus Christ, our God and Savior"* (2 Pet. 1:1 NLT). At the climactic conclusion of scripture, Revelation, we are presented with God's final, unyielding insistence upon holiness and His just dealing with all that does not yield to His holiness. Considering what a central theme this is, it is always surprising when I speak in churches in the West, that so many church members are almost totally unaware of this truth. I think that in part this is because of a false dichotomy that has developed in which, by embracing the mercy of God, we reject his justice. Many see His justice as something belonging to the Old Testament.

When the Bible instructs us to live justly, to do justice, it is enjoining us to treat people equitably and fairly. Justice means to give people what they should rightly have. In both the Old and New Testaments, the original words for justice and righteousness are closely linked, in fact almost synonymous. Justice is something we *do* in order to achieve a righteous state of affairs. When those in a position to exercise authority, do so in a fair manner, this is behaving justly – they are being righteous. God cares deeply about justice. As N.T. Wright has written,

> God's justice is a saving, healing, restorative justice, because the God to whom justice belongs is the Creator God who has yet to complete his original plan for creation and whose justice is designed not simply to restore balance to a world out of kilter but to bring to glorious completion and fruition the creation, teeming with life and possibility, that he made in the first place.[8]

Justice is about God coming to set things right. It is the restoration of life as God intended it to be. As such, justice points back to His original creation and ahead to the culmination of His purposes as Christ returns to establish a new earth (Rev. 21).

George Bernard Shaw once said, "God made man in His image, and ever since then man has been returning the favor." The question, "Who is God?" may be the most important one that we can ever ask because it seems to be a universal truth that we become like what we worship. As we have seen, what we believe about God determines the way we will follow Him and therefore

---

8 N.T. Wright, Evil and the Justice of God (Downers Grove: IVP, 2006), 64.

the way we will live our lives. In order to examine what scripture tells us about justice, and what our response should be, we must first look at the justice that resides in the character of God Himself. God's love of justice and righteousness as well as His hatred of injustice are the reflection of who He is.

God hates idolatry. With our modern perspective, when we hear of idolatry we think of a statue or image that is worshiped. But at its core, idolatry is to believe in a lie about God's character; the idolatrous heart believes that God is other then He really is. That is why God hates it. Idolatry substitutes the true God for one made according to the person or group's preferences. A.W. Tozer wrote: "The essence of idolatry is the entertainment of thoughts about God that are unworthy of Him."[9] Idolatry imagines things about God and then acts as if they were true. The world says, "God is love so He wouldn't allow there to be eternal punishment." However, does this popular and comfortable view reflect the God of the Bible?

God has given us the scriptures as a love letter that reveals His identity and character. *"God has spoken plainly, and I have heard it many times: Power, O God, belongs to You; unfailing love, O Lord, is yours"* (Psa. 62:11–12 NLT). God is both power and love – authority and mercy. If we are not following a God who is both loving and powerful, we are not following the God of the Bible. God needs to be both of these in our lives, or we will struggle with insecurity, either fearing that He does not love us enough to take care of us, or He is not powerful enough to help us and so we must move on our own behalf.

God's mercy flows out of His goodness, and goodness without justice is not goodness. Greg Mitchell has pointed out that justice is God's love toward a victim; mercy is God's love toward a criminal.[10] If there is no justice we are not safe. We are always

---

9 A.W. Tozer, *The Knowledge of the Holy.* New York: Harper & Brothers, 1961), 11.

10 Used by permission.

struggling to believe in a God of love and authority. The Western church too often falls away from this tension, preaching love but not authority, Savior but not Lord. It is almost universally embraced in our society that God is too kind to punish the ungodly. This is a dangerous lie (idolatry) designed to soothe the conscience. Again, Mitchell observes that when God sends people to hell, He is respecting their decision to not have a relationship with Him, because hell is the ultimate place where relationship with God is absent.

THE JUST KING

God's love and concern for the lost does not change His divine holiness into some kind of benign kindness. God's love is a seeking love, but it is also a holy love. He is the heavenly Father (Matt. 6:9), but His name is to be hallowed, to be glorified and to be reverenced. When confronted by the person of Jesus and the message of the Kingdom, every person must make a decision and the outcome of that decision will either be receiving the salvation of the Kingdom or judgment. The truth that God is an inviting Father does not negate or contradict the righteousness and justice of God. The meaning of the Kingdom of God is both salvation and justice.

We have already seen that the New Testament presents Jesus as God coming in His fullness (Col. 1:15ff; Heb. 1:3). Jesus carries the full authority of the Father and shares in His rule over all creation. This extends to the summing up of all things before the throne of God at the end of the Age. The New Testament is very clear on this ultimate reality. *"We must all appear before the judgment seat of Christ"* (2 Cor. 5:10). *"For we will all stand before God's judgment seat"* (Rom. 14:10).

Everyone, all Christians included, will one day stand before the just King, the One who loves and demands justice and hates injustice. Everyone will give an account to the One who in His holiness can never ignore injustice.

Understanding God as the Just King has greatly impacted the way I have presented the gospel over the past several years. As I stand before men and women in cities towns and villages around the developing world, I have become acutely aware of my responsibility to make the gospel unambiguous and to present them with a clear choice: to embrace the King and His Kingdom or to reject His love and holiness.

John 10:10 has become a key text for me: *"The thief comes to steal kill and destroy, but I have come that you might have abundant life."* Everyone must choose either to remain under the control of the thief or to embrace the holy and loving King. There is no third option. That is why I do not "chat" the gospel. That is why I do not give them something that they can chew on and consider in the coming days. When I stand before men and women, I do so fully aware that I may never see them again and that this is my one opportunity to present the gospel of the Kingdom. And so I unabashedly and without apology seek to bring them to the place of crisis. Jesus tells us to choose – and there are eternal ramifications to the choice we make. Jesus was not reluctant to talk about judgment and hell. The King comes as Judge because evil *does* exist and the King confronts it. Part of God's Greater Story is the cosmic battle between the Kingdom of God and the kingdom of darkness. The battle is real, the stakes are eternal and the danger is genuine.

Connected with the justice of the King is His holiness. To avoid talking about the holiness of the King is to present an unreal gospel. Beyond that, if we do not make people aware of the final implications of this battle we present a dull and small gospel. I believe that this is the cause of much apathy and listlessness in the church today. If we have a small king then we have a small kingdom. Jesus is the one who judges the nations, who judges between the sheep and goats. Our God *is* a consuming fire (Heb. 12:29). We really are to work out our salvation with fear and trembling, as Paul tells us (Phil. 2:12).

Perhaps the most well known verse in the New Testament is John 3:16. I believe with all my heart in the great power of the love of God. I've watched this power transform lives in many nations. But it is God's holiness that makes His love so powerful. It is because of our desperate human condition, because of the consequence of our rebellion, that He sent His Son, Jesus. This was not a nice idea, from a benign father. This was a cosmic act of rescue. The just King is also the rescuing King.

It is the holiness and justice of God that reveal the depth and power of His love. Frederick Bruner has written:

> We seek to keep Jesus' hard commands simply because Jesus commands us to do so; we are encouraged by his promise to be with us and to strengthen us (Matt. 28:20); but our seeking will always be inadequate and will always drive us back to the grace of the beatitudes for the needy because of our inescapable weakness in keeping his commandments as they deserve.[11]

The holiness of the just King is every bit as real and powerful as His love. To hide this is to present an incomplete gospel, one that does not authentically present people with the challenge to make a choice. God does not send people to hell; they make that decision themselves. Jesus came to point the way to the seeking, inviting and just Father because He knew the eternal significance of the gospel he presented.

JUSTICE AND
THE CHARACTER OF GOD

---

11 Frederick D. Bruner, *The Christbook Matthew 1–12* (Grand Rapids: Eerdmans, 2007), 204.

Justice is not so much something that God *does;* justice is something that He *is.* Psalm 146 provides a clear picture of the character and just actions of God.

> *[He] executes justice for the oppressed;*
> *who gives food to the hungry.*
> *The LORD sets the prisoners free.*
> *The LORD opens the eyes of the blind;*
> *the LORD raises up those who are bowed down;*
> *the LORD loves the righteous;*
> *the LORD protects the strangers;*
> *He supports the fatherless and the widow,*
> *but He thwarts the way of the wicked.*
> (Psa. 146:7–9 NASB)

Here we see the restoration of life as God intends. When the Kingdom comes (His rule and reign), it comes with justice and who God *is* invades the situation and brings change. His Kingdom and His justice are more all encompassing than we realize. When a blind boy sees, God's justice comes – the boy's life is restored to God's original intention. Likewise when the hungry are fed, when prisoners are liberated, when hope comes to the oppressed, when the most vulnerable people in any society – widows, orphans and aliens – are protected, it is because of who God is, and because His Kingdom has come near. To discover who God really is, is to encounter the Father to the fatherless, the defender of widows, orphans and the powerless (Deut. 10:18; Psa. 68:5). This is what He does because this is who He is. How clear can this be? Our just God loves justice.

> *"For the Lord is righteous and He loves justice. Those who do what is right will see His face"* (Psa. 11:7 NLT).

Notice that His love for justice is expressed with a promise: If we are hungry to experience His manifest presence, then we must learn to love what He loves. God is passionate about justice and He wants His children to be, too. There is no greater promise than to see His face, because His greatest gift to us is always the gift of intimacy. When we get close to someone, we discover who they really are – and it is often a surprise (hopefully, a happy one!). True intimacy with someone also changes us. If we discover that our hearts are beginning to long for justice, we can be encouraged that His heart is changing us.

Justice is God's standard. The Psalmist tells us, *"Your throne is founded on two strong pillars – the one is Justice and the other Righteousness"* (Psa. 89:14 TLB). A couple of years ago I was confronted by a verse in Isaiah: *"I will take the measuring line of justice and the plumb line of righteousness to check the foundation wall you have built"* (Isa. 28:17 NLT).

There are many different kinds of churches – some are built on worship, others on evangelism or preaching. While these and other emphases are good, Isaiah tells us that when God examines our work he is looking for one foundation, and one foundation only: Righteousness and Justice. God is justice and when we love justice, we are in agreement with Him.

The magnificent messianic Psalm 45 is clear:

Your throne, O God, will last for ever and ever;
a scepter of justice will be the scepter of your kingdom.
You love righteousness and hate wickedness;
therefore God, your God,
has set you above your companions
by anointing you with the oil of joy.
(Psa. 45:6–7)

The writer to the Hebrews quotes this passage, declaring the essence of the Son, Jesus Christ. The issue of justice was not peripheral for Jesus, nor was it peripheral to the gospel that the early church proclaimed. As this passage makes clear, when justice is established, the Lord rejoices.

GOD SEES AND HATES INJUSTICE

Jesus taught us to pray, "Our Father, who is in the heavens." Jesus is reminding us that God is our Father and that our Father is all around us. He is over all of life (His transcendence) and He is in the midst of all of life (His imminence and omnipresence). As any father knows, when his children are treated unfairly or when they are attacked something rises up in him. Fathers are first and foremost protectors and defenders of their children. God is never unaware or indifferent to suffering and injustice. He sees it in nations; He sees it in the most remote village; He sees it in every oppressed life. And His passion for His children causes His anger to rise up. Psalm 10:8–15 is just one of many expressions of God's hatred for injustice:

> *[The wicked man] lies in wait near the villages;*
> *from ambush he murders the innocent,*
> *watching in secret for his victims.*
> *He lies in wait like a lion in cover;*
> *he lies in wait to catch the helpless;*
> *he catches the helpless and drags them off in his net.*
> *His victims are crushed, they collapse;*
> *they fall under his strength.*
> *He says to himself, "God has forgotten;*
> *he covers his face and never sees."*
>
> *Arise, LORD! Lift up your hand, O God.*
> *Do not forget the helpless.*
> *Why does the wicked man revile God?*
> *Why does he say to himself,*
> *"He won't call me to account"?*
>
> *But you, O God, do see trouble and grief;*
> *you consider it to take it in hand.*
> *The victim commits himself to you;*

you are the helper of the fatherless.
Break the arm of the wicked and evil man;
call him to account for his wickedness
that would not be found out.

When we, the Father's children and Jesus' disciples, are made aware of injustice and we feel anger and sadness rising up inside, this is simply a sign of God's image within us.

Conversely, a curse rests on us if we withhold justice from others. Proverbs tell us, *"Whoever oppresses a poor man insults his Maker, but he who is generous to the needy honors Him"* (Prov. 14:31 ESV).

These are strong words, reflecting the passion of God. Who among us would ever seek to insult the Lord? Yet He tells us that is exactly what we do if we contribute to the oppression of the poor. While on the surface, our immediate response is likely that we would never contribute to such a thing, but what are we doing when we purchase items at the lowest price we can – clothing from Bangladesh, coffee from west Africa, chocolate, electronics, shoes – even when that low price is the result of unfair labor practices or even slave labor? And closer to home, what about the treatment of immigrants, many of them brought in illegally to work far below a subsistence level of pay? We know about this, but what do we do on their behalf? God addresses the issue of how we treat aliens and strangers almost one hundred times in the scriptures. *"Cursed is the man who withholds justice from the alien, the fatherless or the widow"* (Deut. 27:19). Surely, to know about injustice and yet do nothing is to withhold justice. It is impossible to overstate how serious this is to God.

Jesus' final story in the gospels was about the sheep and the goats (Matt. 25). It is interesting that his strongest words of judgment are for those who saw the poor suffering and yet did nothing. It is clear that "doing justice and loving mercy" are the fruit of a new life in Christ. Jesus clearly told us that we would be known by our fruit. It only makes sense that if we fall in love with Him, His passion will become ours. John 15 tells us that intimacy with Jesus leads to fruitfulness. Micah 6:8 and Matthew 25 reveal the fruit that He wants to see.

God not only hears the cry of the oppressed, He comes to the rescue.

You hear, O LORD, the desire of the afflicted,
you encourage them, and you listen to their cry,
defending the fatherless and the oppressed,
in order that man, who is of the earth,
may terrify no more.
(Psa. 10:17–18)

He will rescue the poor when they cry to him;
he will help the oppressed,
who have no one to defend them.
He feels pity for the weak and the needy,
and he will rescue them.
He will save them from oppression and from violence,
for their lives are precious to him.
(Psa. 72:12–14 NLT)

GOD RESCUES
THROUGH YOU AND ME

This is what the LORD Almighty says: "Administer true justice; show mercy and compassion to one another. Do not oppress the widow or the fatherless, the alien or the poor" (Zech. 7: 9–10).

How does God rescue the poor, the weak, the overlooked? He does it through us, His people. God awakens, envisions and releases us to reflect who He is – the fiery, passionate God of justice and mercy. The early church was known, even by its persecutors, for its rescuing, compassionate acts toward the poor and the weak.

God's message to His church has not changed: Intervene on behalf of the refugee, the single mother, the elderly, the migrant worker, the latch-key children, the homeless. This takes us back to the principle of Matthew 16:19 that whatever *we* release on earth, that is what is released in and from heaven.

God calls us to reflect who He is to the world. So what does the justice of God mean for us?

> *He has showed you, O man, what is good.*
> *And what does the Lord require of you?*
> *To act justly and to love mercy*
> *and to walk humbly with your God.*
> (Mic. 6:8)

How clear this is! When we ask, "God, what do you want from me?" this is His response – Do three things: embrace justice, treasure mercy and walk in humility with Him. When we begin to pursue justice and mercy on behalf of the weak, the poor and the oppressed, we quickly come face-to-face with our limitations and our inconsistencies. And this brings us to the place of humility. Counter-intuitively, humility is very powerful. Humility is the exact opposite of the spirit of the age, spiritual powers and our adversary. When we walk in humility, we find favor and grace coming to us as the enemy retreats. Howard Thurman in his book, *Jesus and the Disinherited,* points out that humility cannot be humiliated.[12] It cannot be attacked or taken away from us from any outside source. Micah 6:8 is the standard and the compass point for following Jesus.

• • •

Once when I was in Nicaragua with a team from Impact Nations, we were conducting a medical clinic in a small village. It is always

12 Howard Thurman, *Jesus and the Disinherited* (Boston: Beacon Press, 1976), 27.

surprising to see the level of abject poverty existing only a short flight away from the affluence of North America. During the day a few hundred of the villagers received medical care. That evening we gathered in one of the lane ways with songs, street dramas and an opportunity for them to hear about and experience Jesus and His Kingdom. While the music was playing I was brought to the community leader. She told me that there were only a few shallow wells, and these with unsafe water, resulting in water-borne disease for many in the village. She also told me there was a water line on the edge of town through which flowed safe water; however, they could not access it because they could not afford the pipes. When I found out that the cost of the pipe was only $240, I asked the team if they would be willing to give in order to make this happen. Their answer was an enthusiastic 'Yes.'

We in the West do not realize how much can be accomplished with what we would consider a small amount of money, but which is an unattainable amount in much of the developing world. When I told the village leader that we would be pleased to provide the pipe, she began to call out this good news to the several hundred who had gathered. A huge cheer went up and some even began to dance. The gospel is meant to be good news to the poor.

Two weeks later I was sent pictures of the villagers digging trenches for the water pipes. I was deeply touched to see them laboring in the heat. Our contribution was the easy part; theirs required the real work. Later one of our team went back to that village in Nicaragua. There are now faucets about every hundred feet. He watched people continuously coming and filling their containers. The best part was when the village leader told my friend that the sickness which had plagued this village for years was now gone. She also told him that she and others had been praying for a long time for God to intervene in the village. God rescues the poor, and He uses us to do so.

A LIVING HOPE

We are called to bring a living hope (1 Pet. 1:3). The gospel is powerful enough to reach into the darkness of injustice and turn lives around. Hope is a powerful force that unlocks the dreams and potential that God puts into every person. Bringing hope to the poor and the oppressed is one of the great joys of following Jesus. Currently, each year Impact Nations conducts thirty-five to forty mobile medical clinics in remote villages and urban slums around the developing world. During the orientation training, my wife, Christina, will often pick up a small bag of medicine or vitamins and ask the team members "Do you know what this is? This is 'hope in a bag.'" I think it is because I see the power of hope among the poor again and again that I try to keep pressing forward. Often very small acts produce great results. When the impoverished mother living in a small village with her children suddenly discovers that she is not invisible, that someone does care, this in itself stirs "a living hope."

Seeking to bring hope and justice to the poor does not happen without a lot of pain and disappointment; it is a tumultuous adventure, but an adventure nevertheless. David Bosch in his book, *Transforming Mission*, gives a wonderful definition of this living hope:

> Christian hope is both possession and the yearning, repose and activity, arrival and being on the way. Since God's victory is certain, believers can work both patiently and enthusiastically, blending careful planning with urgent obedience, motivated by the patient impatience of the Christian hope.[13]

A prophetic church is much more than one where people stand up

---

13 David J. Bosch, *Transforming Mission: Paradigm Shifts in Theology of Mission* (Maryknoll, NY: Obis, 1991), n.p.

on a Sunday morning and prophesy (though certainly that is one part). The prophetic church declares what God's standard is and in doing so, highlights the dynamic tension between God's standard and our actions.

Jim Wallis, in his book, *God's Politics*, writes about the choice to be a prophetic people:

> Prophetic faith does not see the primary battle as the struggle between belief and secularism. It understands that the real battle, the big struggle of our times, is the fundamental choice between cynicism and hope. The prophets always begin in judgment, in a social critique of the status quo, but they end in hope – that these realities can and will be changed.[14]

It is easy to simply criticize what is wrong. It takes no faith or prophetic sense to see a valley of dry bones (Ezek. 37). But it takes the heart of God beating in us, to look at those bones and see an army coming to life. That is the prophetic role of the church. We agree with God who *"calls forth the things that are not as though they were"* (Rom. 4:17). A prophetic church not only declares God's standard to the world around it; it intercedes on behalf of people suffering from injustice, confident that in doing so the church is opening the door for "justice to roll on like a river."

Walter Wink in his book, *The Powers That Be,* says that intercession "is spiritual defiance of what is, in the name of what God has promised"[15]. Jesus continues to challenge us in this day with His admonition that we have not because we ask not. The prophetic church stands before God on behalf of people and declares not only that things must change, but also that its declaration is part of initiating the very change it desires to see.

---

14 Jim Wallis, *God's Politics* (New York: HarperCollins, 2005), 346.

15 Walter Wink, *The Powers That Be* (New York: Doubleday, 1998), 185.

This kind of intercession changes history because it believes the future into being. The apostle Paul tells the Romans that all of creation is groaning and waiting. Creation is waiting for this kind of forceful prophetic declaration and prayer that refuses to take no for an answer, that stands up in the face of injustice and creates the very future it sees by agreeing with God and His Kingdom.

As Christians, our citizenship is in heaven and we are more than invited – we are exhorted through this forceful, aggressive prayer to pull the reality of heaven into this world. Prophetic prayer is aggressive prayer that makes demands, knowing that it is in agreement with the will of God. Through this kind of intercession we are co-creators with God. Forceful men and women take hold of the Kingdom and that is why Jesus tells us to keep on asking, keep on seeking and keep on knocking. *"Do not give Him [the Lord] any rest until He establishes Jerusalem and makes it an object of praise throughout the earth"* (Isa. 62:7 GWT).

STANDING IN THE GAP

I looked for someone who might rebuild the wall of righteousness that guards the land. I searched for someone to stand in the gap in the wall so I wouldn't have to destroy the land, but I found no one (Ezek. 22:30 NLT).

This well-known passage is most typically quoted in the context of intercession, referring to God's search for those who pray. While this is certainly true, this verse must be examined in light of its context. The prophet Ezekiel is pointing out victims of injustice and oppression, saying that God is looking for someone to act on their behalf.

Your princes plot conspiracies just as lions stalk their prey. They devour innocent people, seizing treasures and extorting wealth. They make many widows in the land ... Your leaders are like wolves, who tear apart their victims.

They actually destroy people's lives for money! ... Even common people oppress the poor, rob the needy, and deprive foreigners of justice ... I searched for someone to stand in the gap (Ezek. 22:25–30 NLT).

We must pray *and* we must act. Authentic intercession always takes us from the prayer room into the world. I encourage intercessors to step out, believing that God has heard their prayers and will respond.

In Luke 18 Jesus told the story of a persistent widow who continued to cry out to the judge for justice until she finally got what she demanded. In verse seven Jesus says this: *"Will not God bring about justice for His chosen ones, who cry out to Him day and night?"* This is the heart of the persistent prayer to which God calls the church – the cry for justice in the world: the restoration of life as God intended.

God is passionate about justice; as we cry out to Him on behalf of the poor and oppressed, as we give ourselves to His great cause, the reality of His Kingdom begins to do its transformative work.

11

GOD'S JUSTICE
IN THE WORLD

Your throne, O God, will last forever and ever; a scepter
of justice will be the scepter of Your Kingdom. You love
righteousness and hate wickedness.   PSALM 45:6

As we have seen, when Jesus announced that the Kingdom of
God had come, He was declaring that the rule and reign of God,
the power and reality of heaven, was penetrating this present age.
The ultimate reality of God's Kingdom has come to earth. And
when the Kingdom comes, it comes with justice. Justice is the
restoration of life as God intended it to be; it is the restoration of
what is broken. Because of this I understand justice to be about
societal and national restoration; but it is also about the rescue and
the restoration of a single life. For this reason, I see the ministry
of healing in the context of justice because it is the restoration of
what has been taken away from someone. When the little boy in
Uganda had his withered arm instantly healed, that was justice –
God restored to him the life he always intended for that boy. When
a village in the Philippines gets clean water, that too is justice.

As noted earlier, Jesus began his public ministry in his
hometown by reading from Isaiah 61:

> *The Spirit of the Lord is upon me,*
> *because he has anointed me*

to bring good news to the poor.
He has sent me to proclaim release to the captives
and recovery of sight to the blind,
to let the oppressed go free,
to proclaim the year of the Lord's favor.
(Luke 4:18–19)

This is His Magna Carta; it is the closest that Jesus ever came to a mission statement. His proclamation not only announces release, but is also the initial step in bringing about divine intervention and deliverance. From the beginning, Jesus both *announced* and *demonstrated* the Kingdom of God. Jesus underlined this truth when, after reading these verses from Isaiah 61, He gave the examples of the prophets Elijah and Elisha who both demonstrated the power of God through miraculous interventions. From the beginning, this gospel was not just something to believe and talk about – it has always demanded faith put into action. This mission statement is holistic, impacting every aspect of life, individually and socially.

THE KINGDOM AND JUBILEE

I am indebted to Christopher Wright for his observations and insights on the Jubilee in his book, *The Mission of God*.[16]

When Jesus announced the year of the Lord's favor, every one of His listeners would have known that He was referring to the year of Jubilee, a time when inequalities throughout the nation were removed. Leviticus 25 lays out the principles and parameters of the year of Jubilee. At its heart, Jubilee is about restoration and liberty. Every 50th year, Israelites who had become slaves because of their indebtedness were set free. Land that had been sold by families because of economic hardship was restored to them. This

16 Christopher Wright, *The Mission of God* (Downers Grove: IVP, 2006).

was a year of Sabbath for the whole nation, which included leaving the land fallow for the entire year. Obedience to this law required great trust and dependence upon the provision of the Lord.

The returning of land to its original owners and the forgiveness of debt highlight God's desire for His people. Firstly, Jubilee brought about a basic equality of opportunity. Families received back land according to their size and need. Jesus taught this to His followers when He told them to give to the one who asks and to share food and clothing. The early church obviously embraced this Jubilee principle. *"All the believers were united in heart and mind. And they felt that what they owned was not their own, so they shared everything they had"* (Acts 4:32 TLB).

Secondly, the land was kept, as much as possible, within the extended family; it was not merely a commodity to be sold to the highest bidder. Thirdly, the land belonged to God. This is a truth that runs through the scriptures. *"The land really belongs to me, so you can't sell it for all time. You are only foreigners and travelers living for a while on my land"* (Lev. 25:23 NCV).

God's people were (and are) commissioned by Him to be faithful stewards, caring for land that is under God's ownership. Jesus may have had this in mind when He told the local leaders to render to God the things that are His (Mark 12:17). Jubilee was a tangible reminder with powerful economic and social implications that we are invited into a life of trusting service to a faithful God. Fourthly, Israelites were to live this life as travelers and aliens. This was a theme that was reiterated throughout the New Testament (see Heb. 11:13; 1 Pet. 1:1; Phil. 3:20).

At its heart, Jubilee brought real hope for change. No wonder Jesus announced the Kingdom of God as "the year of the Lord's favor." Isaiah 61 is a prophetic vision of the coming renewal of life. It expresses the marks of Jubilee and of the Kingdom: the rich give to the poor, captives are freed, the eyes of the blind are opened. Jubilee not only brings hope for the *future*, but also makes ethical demands in the *present*. The early church did not respond to this future hope by simply waiting, praying for God to break in; they proactively put the ethics of Jubilee/Kingdom into practice. The result was a new kind of community. In this way they lived prophetically as a signpost of the Kingdom of God coming in its fullness. It was a community marked by social and financial equality. And because it was moving in the rhythm of life as God intended it to be – spiritually, socially, economically – they experienced a favor that caused the church to grow in strength and numbers.

There is a new reality. It is an all-encompassing reality. We err when we limit our understanding and expectation of Jubilee/the Kingdom of God to either spiritual realities (like healing, salvation and spiritual renewal in the church) or to sociopolitical and economic re-structuring. Forgiveness (release) is both spiritual forgiveness of sin *and* financial release from actual debt. Therefore, Jubilee challenges us to bring forth the fruits of repentance, of experiencing the forgiveness of God. For Jubilee/Kingdom people, "as we forgive our debtors" means an opportunity to express practically and economically what we have received.

Perhaps the largest issue in history to which Jubilee speaks is international debt. Just as the gap between the rich and the poor has been widening every year in North America, so has the gap between rich and poor nations. Along with unfair trade policies, international debt is the major cause of this incredible disparity. Although the actual figures vary according to how they are gathered, *all* research shows the following:

Since the 1970s, poor nations have paid more in interest than they have received in funds, yet their current debt has not substantially diminished. One study indicates that African nations have received $540 billion in loans, have paid back $550 billion, and yet have a current outstanding balance of $295 billion.[17]

---

17 <http://www.jubileeusa.org/truth-about-debt/why-drop-the-debt.

For every $1 that African nations receive in loans, they pay $2.30 in debt service.

When examining grants to African nations, the gap is even wider; for every $1 received, they pay $13 in interest.

For many poor countries, servicing the debt owed to "have" nations means no health care and limited education for their citizens. National debt traps them in a holding pattern of poverty and hopelessness. Jubilee and the Kingdom of God demand that such great inequities be corrected and the poor not be abandoned. In 2005, just over half of Zambia's debt of $7.1 billion was forgiven. Remember, they had been paying interest on that debt for decades. Having traveled to Zambia on two occasions, I have seen the huge impact this has had on her people. Firstly, with freedom from much of this crushing burden of debt, the Zambian government was able to provide full health care for all of its rural citizens, most of whom previously had to walk one or two days to reach understaffed clinics in hope of getting treatment for children dying of cerebral malaria, endemic to the area. Secondly, the government was able to hire forty-five hundred new teachers. Education is the key to whether or not a nation advances.

Like Jesus and His disciples, embracing Jubilee means both living as a new community and being a prophetic people who declare and insist upon *"justice, mercy and faithfulness"* (Matt. 23:23). Jesus consistently taught in accordance with this new Jubilee order. For example, just as Israel was commanded to leave the land fallow for a year, Jesus told His listeners not to be anxious about the necessities of life – about being fed, clothed and sheltered (Matt. 6:25–34).

As citizens of an occupied nation in the first century, most rural landowners were living under the burden of both Rome's and Herod's heavy tax demands. As a result, most of them had lost their independence; forced to mortgage their property just to

html>.

pay the taxes, they were reduced to a type of slavery. The same situation exists today in the developing world where millions are enslaved by unjust and impossible debt demands. It was in this environment that Jesus told His followers to forgive debts, to lend freely expecting nothing in return, assuring them that their reward would be great and they would be sons of the Most High (Luke 6:32–36).

Like many people, I wrestle with the radical demands of discipleship. Jesus really *does* expect me to live under a whole new standard. And the more I study what Jesus really said in the gospels, the more challenged (and if I am honest, disturbed) I become. Jesus was totally committed to the Kingdom of God and He challenges us to follow Him in that radical commitment.

The Kingdom of God, Jubilee, has an irresistible, unstoppable force to it. The Kingdom carries its own life and energy. Jesus said that it is like yeast, and though it starts very small, it carries with it all the energy of heaven and so it grows and grows. While the church is called to express the Kingdom of God on earth, the Kingdom is bigger than the church. It touches every aspect of life and wherever it is embraced it advances. When the Kingdom comes, it brings inexorable change. Because of the power and reality of the Kingdom, justice *will* flow like a river. Martin Luther King once said, "The moral arc of the universe is long, but it bends toward justice."[18] Though powerful and profoundly unjust forces pressed against him, Dr. King knew that the Kingdom of God must prevail, because God loves justice and hates injustice. One hundred years ago Mahatma Gandhi saw in Christ's Sermon on the Mount the irresistible power of justice. This Sermon became the compass point for Gandhi as he called the nation of India to nonviolent resistance against the British Empire. It is likely that Gandhi was not a Christian in any traditional sense (although there

---

18 Martin Luther King Jr., *Our God is Marching On, Testament of Hope* (New York: HarperCollins, 1986), 230.

has been significant discussion about this) but the principles of the Kingdom are universal and powerful. In the natural, India's situation seemed impossible; all of the power was in the hands of the British. So why did India gain its independence? Martin Luther King was right: no matter how long the battle, the universe bends toward justice, because God loves justice. God is committed to bringing "release to the captives and letting the oppressed go free."

At the heart of being the people who reflect the justice of their Father, is the deep conviction that He tells us that we are here to make a difference – more than that, to partner with Him in bringing about justice and rescuing lives. As a young man I remember hearing my pastor, Vic Gledhill, say this: "The Father has a family, the family has a business, and that business is people." I have repeated this to congregations and leaders in many nations. The family business is about justice and the Kingdom of God. And it is about bringing these to people. Disciples of Jesus are never permitted to live out their discipleship theoretically. After all is not theoretical discipleship an oxymoron? Disciples are called to action. Disciples are called to put hands and feet to the gospel.

• • •

Earlier, I wrote briefly about some sewing schools that Impact Nations helped to start in various villages in South India. These were not started simply in order to help someone improve the standard of living for women. Rather, what motivated us was a deep desire to come head on against cultural and generational injustice. In many ways going into these villages is like stepping back in time, not only because of the lack of modern amenities, but because they are locked in the rigid and oppressive caste system. As is usual throughout the developing world, the women and their children are at the bottom of the pecking order. Most girls receive little or no meaningful education; typically, they begin working in the fields at seven or eight years of age. In their culture, marriages are arranged and very often a girl as young as twelve or thirteen will find herself being married to a much, much older man. Fathers will marry off their daughters in this way largely for economic reasons; they simply cannot afford to continue to feed unmarried daughters. All too often, the older husbands die leaving teenage girls as widows. Four thousand years of tradition dictate that these young widows be expelled from the home and even from the village, leaving them with almost no options for survival except begging, prostitution or – if they are fortunate – working twelve-hour days in the fields for about one dollar a day. They are completely ostracized, since crossing paths with a widow in this culture is considered bad luck. Many of these young girls despair of life, some even choosing to commit suicide. This is the kind of injustice that God hates, against which He calls us to stand.

Ravathi was twelve years old when her father arranged her marriage to a much older man; and so she went to live with her unknown husband and his family. When she was fourteen, Ravathi had a baby. Immediately upon the child's birth, her husband's sister took the baby away and killed it. I cannot even imagine the pain of that for this young mother. A year later Ravathi was pregnant again. This time her in-laws forced her to have an abortion. One year after that her husband died. Ravathi was expelled from the home, but not before being told that in fact her husband had been HIV positive, and now so too was Ravathi. Then, everything changed. One of my Indian friends encountered Ravathi sleeping at the edge of the field and invited her home to where a growing number of widows and orphans were now beginning to gather. Ravathi entered the six-month sewing school program. She did so well that she was invited to stay on as an instructor for the next school.

Jhoti was also a widow who had been cast out of her home and village. In her despair she jumped down a well; however, she was seen as she did this and was rescued. Like many other poor village women, Jhoti had never received the schooling necessary to learn to read or write. She too was invited into one of the early sewing schools and like Ravathi, she excelled. Upon graduation she started her own home business. This was a very gifted lady; she was able to obtain a contract to make clothing for a company in Hyderabad. Not only this, Jhoti also began her own school.

Injustice robbed both of these women of the potential that God had put in them. The Kingdom of God came to their lives and once again everything changed. But what blossomed was what had always been there, simply waiting for the opportunity of expression. One of the greatest nights of my life occurred when I attended the graduation of the first two sewing classes. Under colourful lights and surrounded by family members and even dignitaries, eighty heroic young women proceeded to the front (dressed in the graduation gowns that each had made themselves) to the sound of thunderous applause. These women, most of whom came to the school not knowing even how to read or write, these women who had been held down and ignored for most of their lives were no longer invisible. As I watched them come forward I was aware of their determination. But I was also aware that something had profoundly changed. These women had not only learned how to sew and run a home business, every one of them in an atmosphere of love and encouragement had discovered that they had great value because God values them. Besides this, they made the greatest discovery of all: Although about eighty-five percent of the women who came to the school were Hindus and Muslims (the Kingdom is for everybody), at every school, *every one* of these amazing women encountered Jesus and gave their lives joyfully to Him. And with this discovery they walked forward with a dignity they had never known before.

One of the passages that I remember being taught on several occasions as a young man was Isaiah 1:18: *"Come, let us reason together; though your sins be as scarlet they will become as white as snow."* This of course is a wonderful passage that encourages us to come in faith to Christ, believing that He will wash us clean. But once again, the context is that of bringing the justice of God to those in need. *"Seek justice, encourage the oppressed. Defend the cause of the fatherless, plead the case of the widow. Come, let us reason together ..."* (Isa. 1:17–18). These words resonated inside me as one after another, these heroic women came forward to receive their diplomas.

JUSTICE AND RESPONSIBLE LEADERSHIP

As we have seen, Jesus was declaring God's liberty and restoration in the tradition of the year of Jubilee, established by God and to be adhered to by a theocratic society. We must remember that Jesus was addressing an occupied nation with most of the people living under systems of political and economic oppression. How are we, as His disciples and as members of His new community, to live prophetically?

At the height of Solomon's reign, God brought the Queen of Sheba to prophesy over him.

> *Praise be the Lord your God who has delighted in you and placed you on the throne of Israel. Because of the Lord's eternal love for Israel, He has made you king to maintain justice and righteousness* (1 Kings 10:9).

The responsibility of political leadership is to release the blessing of justice to people. This goes all the way back to Abraham.

> *For I have chosen him, so that he may command his children and his household after him to keep the way of the LORD by doing righteousness and justice, so that the LORD may bring upon Abraham what He has spoken about him* (Gen. 18:19–20 NASB).

In his book, *Generous Justice*, Timothy Keller uses two very helpful terms in describing justice. Rectifying justice means punishing those who do wrong and caring for those who are victims of injustice. Primary justice is righteous living. It is "day-to-day living in which a person conducts all relationships in family and society with fairness, generosity and equity."[19]

Job was a contemporary of Abraham. Though not a ruler like Solomon, Job was a social and economic leader in his city who understood the responsibility that comes with leadership. In this passage from Job, we see him operating in both spheres of justice to which Keller refers.

> *Whoever heard me spoke well of me,*
> *and those who saw me commended me,*
> *because I rescued the poor who cried for help*
> *and the fatherless who had none to assist him.*
> *The man who was dying blessed me;*
> *I made the widow's heart sing.*
> *I put on righteousness as my clothing;*
> *justice was my robe and my turban.*
> *I was eyes to the blind and feet to the lame.*
> *I was a father to the needy;*
> *I took up the case of the stranger.*
> *I broke the fangs of the wicked*
> *and snatched the victims from their teeth.*
> (Job 29:11–17)

This is one of the most beautiful and remarkable passages about the blessing of God flowing through those who pursue justice on behalf of the poor and the weak. The poor are helped, the orphans are defended and there is a place for the stranger (illegal immigrant /the undocumented migrant). God is very, very serious about how governments and leaders treat the poor, the widow, the orphan and the alien.

---

19 Timothy Keller: *Generous Justice* (New York: Penguin Group USA, 2010), chapter 1: "What Is Doing Justice?"

Job is a wonderful model for us. God had raised him up as a city leader whose voice people heeded. Job understood his responsibility before God to live justly in his city. He confronted wickedness head-on, likely challenging those who exploited the vulnerable through unfair lending practices and unequal treatment under the law; in other words, the same issues that the poor face today. He was a proactive rescuer of the poor, the sick and the dying.

In Verse 14 Job uses poetic language to say that he was always accutely aware of issues of justice all around him. When our eyes are opened to the issues of injustice and the plight of the poor, at first we are surprised that we have not always seen the poor all around us. From this begins a creativity that reflects the Lord's heart as we begin to develop strategies and interventions – just like Job did. Some of these will take us to the nations; others will take us across town to the single mothers, the new immigrants, the elderly shut-ins and to the latchkey children whose family poverty causes them to live most of their days alone.

The last great King of Judah was Josiah. Through his devotion to God and his commitment to live out His Word, Josiah turned the nation from its apostasy. Many years later, speaking to a captive people now in Babylon, Jeremiah prophesied:

> *This is what the Lord says: be fair minded and just. Do what is right! Help those who have been robbed; rescue them from their oppressors … Do not mistreat foreigners, orphans and widows … [Josiah] was just and right in all his dealings. That is why God blessed him. He gave justice and help to the poor and needy, and everything went well for him. Isn't that what it means to know Me?. says the Lord* (Jer. 22:3, 15–16 NLT).

God looks closely at governments and leaders of all kinds. He looks to see justice and when He sees it, He finds it irresistible. When a nation, region or town is pursuing justice within its borders, God releases His favor. Even at national levels, God resists the proud, but gives grace to the humble. Where we, as His ambassadors, see leaders ruling justly, we have the opportunity to encourage and celebrate what they are doing.

This passage finishes with a very powerful truth: Not only will things go well for us in any sphere of leadership when we pay close attention to the needs of the poor, but God says that this is a primary sign that we really know Him. True intimacy with Him increases our heart for the poor and the oppressed. This is because intimacy always brings us closer to the true heart of the one we pursue; and God's heart is with the poor and the oppressed.

Justice requires a vivid awareness of its centrality in the heart of God so impacting and discomforting, that it propels us to change direction and to take action. If we believe the Bible, both its directives and examples, we must come to the conclusion that our actions *do* effect change. Over the years I have watched as men and women come to the empowering conclusion that they can do more and do it faster than they ever imagined. Always, God has both invited and commanded men and women to uphold His passion for justice. When we believe God, and then let that belief direct our actions, there is a powerful favor that comes.

Biblical righteousness and justice are not concepts, they are lifestyle decisions – decisions with cosmic, eternal consequences.

12

JUSTICE AND THE NEW COMMUNITY

Pure and genuine religion in the sight of God the Father means caring for orphans and widows in their distress and refusing to let the world corrupt you. JAMES 1:27 NLT

When the Kingdom of God comes, it comes with justice. God's restoration is making right what is wrong. The church was established in the heart of God to bring a tangible expression of His Kingdom to the world. The early church was passionate about its call to care for the poor, the widow and the orphan. Before His crucifixion, Jesus had been very clear that His followers were to provide food, clothing and shelter, and to visit those in prison. Jesus was so serious about this that He told his disciples that in doing so they would actually be ministering directly to Him. This was a serious message, and recognizing it as such, the early church gave Jesus' words a great priority. Church historians tell us that the early church was famous for its generosity; believers not only shared with each other as each one had need, but also generously gave to those outside the church. How generous? Some historians suggest that the early church gave away ninety percent and only kept ten percent for its own needs. Even in the midst of its persecution of the church, Rome acknowledged and respected the church's commitment to the poor. Church father Ignatius said that if the church is not marked by caring for the poor, the oppressed and the hungry, then it is guilty of heresy.[20]

There is a great longing for revival today in the Western Church, and I join with that longing, confident that God loves to revive His church. But I fear that in our day we have too small a view of revival. For many of us it means churches packed full, many people making professions of faith, or stadiums filled with large Christian events. These are all good, but they are too small a vision of revival and are not consistent with what it has historically looked like.

True revival has always brought about social change. The Wesleyan revival in England during the eighteenth century was marked by not only its preaching; the crowds gathering from all social classes; and by deep repentance. It was also the revival of a great social conscience. It has been said that the Wesleyan revival saved England from the horrors of the kind of revolution that took place in France. Not only did men and women come to Christ, but fire was awakened to bring justice and transformation in English society. As the Kingdom went forward, there was restoration of life as God intended. In the years following Wesley's death, as a direct result of the revival in which God used him and others to bring to England, the slave trade was stopped, prison reform for both men and women took place, and child labor laws were changed to abolish abusive and inhumane working conditions for children. It may even be said that the sweeping changes that took place with the Reform Act of 1832 found their genesis in the Wesleyan revival. This is the kind of revival for which we must cry out to God, knowing deep in our hearts that He will bring about justice as we cry out to Him (Luke 18:7).

If the church is going to live in agreement with the Word of God, she must actively embrace what God says about the poor and His response to injustice. It is not enough to give mental or

20 Shane Claiborne, *The Irresistible Revolution* (Grand Rapids: Zondervan, 2006), 332.

theological assent to what God says about the poor, yet not let His word direct our priorities as a church. To hear his word and not put it into practice is to build our churches upon sand. After all, this is surely what Jesus meant in the Sermon on the Mount. The movement in the gospels is from concept to activation. John 1:14 tells us that the word became flesh and dwelt among us. That which was in the heart of the Father from before the beginning of time was actualized when He sent Jesus to us. As E. Stanley Jones has put it, "The ideal became real."

Jesus addressed the religious leaders in Matthew 9:13. *"Go and learn what this means, I desire mercy and not sacrifice."* It is so easy for our church programs and our plans to gradually choke out what Jesus said are His priorities (the parable of the sower is for all of us, all the time). Religion is a powerful force that so easily creeps in to all our lives. Over the years I have heard Matthew 23:23 preached as a proof text for tithing:

> *Woe to you, teachers of the law and Pharisees, you hypocrites! You give a tenth of your spices – mint, dill and cumin. But you have neglected the more important matters of the law – justice, mercy and faithfulness. You should have practiced the latter, without neglecting the former.*

The point is made that we should not neglect the tithe. My point is not to enter into the debate of whether or not the New Testament calls for tithing, or whether New Testament giving is a different, higher standard. My point is that once again Jesus was telling the religious leaders to open their eyes and see the bigger picture: that God wants His church filled with justice, mercy and faithfulness.

This chapter began with Amos 5:24, *"Let justice roll on like a river, and righteousness like a never-failing stream."* This verse is powerful and well known, but its context is a stinging indictment of when religion creeps into church life and chokes out God's stated passion and purpose that *"Good News is [be] preached to the poor."* These verses, powerfully captured in The Message, reflect how God feels when the church's values and priorities come into conflict with His. These are strong words indeed:

> *"I can't stand your religious meetings.*
> *I'm fed up with your conferences and conventions.*
> *I want nothing to do with your religion projects,*
> *your pretentious slogans and goals.*
> *I'm sick of your fund-raising schemes,*
> *your public relations and image making.*
> *I've had all I can take of your noisy ego-music.*
> *When was the last time you sang to me?*
> *Do you know what I want?*
> *I want justice – oceans of it.*
> *I want fairness – rivers of it.*
> *That's what I want. That's all I want."*
> (Amos 5:21–24 MSG)

In these words I hear both holy anger and deep sadness. God grieves over the plight of the poor, and I am convinced that He is saddened when we do not carry the same burden. If the church is going to represent and follow Jesus it must be actively connected to the poor. Most typically, middle-class Western churches have very limited interaction with the needy. While many churches have a monthly or even weekly outreach to street people or participate in soup kitchens (which are highly valuable activities) the reality is that these are programs that typically involve only a few dedicated church members. Rarely is there an integrated strategy for significantly connecting, encouraging and helping the poor in our cities. Likewise, rarely is there a theology of justice and the poor taught from the pulpit.

YOU WILL ALWAYS HAVE THE POOR WITH YOU

When I talk about justice and the poor with Christians, not much time goes by before someone reminds me that Jesus said we will have the poor with us always. This is usually expressed as a justification for giving priority to other things. Again, context is vital for understanding the passage. Jesus and His disciples are having a meal at the home of Simon the leper. Many commentators believe that Jesus had healed Simon of leprosy and that He and His disciples were having a meal with a leper who was now "clean." If indeed Simon was still suffering from leprosy, then we see yet again the power of the radical inclusiveness of Jesus' life. While eating the meal, a woman comes in with a flask of very expensive ointment and pours it over Jesus. This extravagant act of worship offended some of the disciples who felt that the money spent to provide this perfume could have been given to the poor. Jesus gently rebukes them and says that what the woman has done is beautiful and will be remembered for all time. It is at this point that He says, "The poor you will have with you always." For three years the disciples had watched and learned as day after day Jesus led them among the poor, the lonely and the outcast – visiting, eating with them and including them. All this time they had seen Him identifying actively with some of the poorest members of an occupied nation. At this point Jesus was simply declaring the reality of being a disciple. Jesus' actions and lifestyle were obedient to what God told Israel in Deuteronomy 15: *"There will never cease to be poor in the land. Therefore I command you, you shall open wide your hand to your brother, to the needy and to the poor, in your land"* (Deut. 15:11).

Jesus said that the gospel is good news to the poor and that we as His disciples, as His church, are to be those who both declare and demonstrate this good news. But how can we bring good news to those with whom we have such limited contact? I believe that for most of us, "having the poor with us always" requires us to be very intentional. What would happen if we taught and encouraged each of our church members to develop at least one friendship among the poor in our community? It is interesting that historically most revivals have begun among the poor and have disproportionately gathered in the poor. I think this is because the poor know their needs more acutely. Many have discovered that in the midst of their poverty, God blesses them with the reality of His Kingdom (Luke 6:20). We must always remember that when the Kingdom comes, it comes with tangible signs (Matt. 11:4–5); and one of these signs is that the good news is proclaimed and demonstrated to the poor.

Very few people would argue that the church should not look out for the poor; however, to activate this principle means to personalize it. If the poor will be with us always, then we must build relationships with them. This is one of the main reasons that Impact Nations takes people from all over the Western world into remote villages and urban slums in the developing world. Not only do we want these "journeyers" to discover that God will use them to heal the sick and lead people to Jesus, we want them to have a personal experience of daily interacting with some of the poorest people anywhere. If this interaction takes place, perceptions begin to change from issues of injustice to actual people. We discover that we need them every bit as much as they need us. As the poor become individual people with individual personalities and dreams, hopes and challenges, the walls in our own hearts begin to come down. Jesus told us that they are our brothers, sisters and mothers (Matt. 12:50). As we realize that this is more than a Bible verse, it becomes a transformational reality in our own lives.

Often I see two things happen as a result of these journeys. Many people, upon returning to their homes in the West, are of course impacted with the incredible contrast; this is the classic "culture shock" of missions. However, God has also planted a holy dissatisfaction in their hearts and they know they will not be the same. The outworking of this is very often that they begin to go out to the poor in their own cities and towns, to see for the first time those who previously were invisible to them. Secondly, sometimes

I am amazed to discover that out of meeting "family members" in Africa, India or Central America that a team member will find a way to keep in touch and to work hand in hand with a villager to bring about sustainable change in his or her situation. Impact team members have worked to help start small businesses; for example, a fritter (a type of fried donut) business that immediately employed desperately poor people who had no capital, but a great dream. Another journeyer returned home and began to tell others her dream of helping a Ugandan woman start a hairdressing salon in her town that would provide income to feed hungry children – and job training for orphan teens. Another journeyer with business experience in the technology field, along with his African friend, has started an Internet café that employs several young men, connects a rural community to the global village and whose profits provide food for orphans.

Impact Nations has created a new kind of website that we call the Impact Network. It is designed to connect people in the West directly with those in the developing world. We become the catalyst to bring them together and then we get out of the way. Through this vehicle, people on both sides of the world can work together to bring about transformational change. A member of the West will hear through the network about a specific project designed to bring about sustainable change. Through the network they communicate directly with our partners on the ground. This makes giving to the poor personal and interactive, and allows for partnership and creativity in developing new solutions. Through our partners on the ground we regularly have opportunities to get Bio-sand filters into small communities in the Philippines. We simply let that be known to the network and then sit back and watch what happens. Inevitably people from around the world donate the money for water filters. Sixty-nine dollars will provide a filter that will give a family clean water for life. But here is where it gets interesting. We have had people donate a filter from North America or Europe on a

Monday and received a photograph and report from a village in the jungle on Wednesday night. Often this leads to an ongoing back-and-forth discussion between East and West as donors receive progress reports directly from the field and then begin to inquire as to what else could be done to further help the community. In the twenty-first century, proximity to the poor can realistically take place from one's living room.

For more than twenty years, one of my most pleasurable experiences in ministry has been the privilege of taking members from different churches out to minister to the poor in their cities. No matter how many times I have done this, it is always exciting to see something new come alive in men, women and children as they go out together, often for the first time, to demonstrate the Kingdom among the poor. In 2009, after teaching what the Bible says about justice and the poor, I went with a church to the poorest housing project in their city. It was filled with immigrants, some refugees, many single mothers (the modern widow) and children of all ages. Usually, when a church goes out for the first time, there is some hesitation and shyness; therefore I was prepared upon arrival to really encourage and exhort them in the parking lot and try to get as many as possible to connect with the people in the housing project with some bags of fruit and offers to pray. However, before I could even get out of the car they scattered around the complex with great enthusiasm. I felt like Gandhi who once said, "There go my people and I must follow, for I am their leader!" The morning itself was very exciting with many people healed, including the total healing of a woman with a blind eye, and a woman who had been bedridden with incapacitating back pain who, after prayer, was running and jumping up and down. During the morning, people gave their lives to Christ (including two young drug dealers). This was very exciting for the church. But something perhaps even more significant happened that morning: the church became connected meaningfully with a community in need, and as they did, something came alive in them. The power of living hope began to move through that community. No longer did the church think of this place as a housing complex; now they were friends, brothers and sisters, on a journey together. From that time to this the power of the gospel is transforming lives, both in the housing community and in the church. Good news to the poor has meant warm hats and mittens for the children in the winter; it has meant providing a bed for a mother who had been sleeping on the floor for months; it has meant helping an Asian immigrant process papers so that the family can be reunited after seven years; it has meant community dinners; and it has also meant a deep and profound awakening in the members of that church as they discover that by "doing justice, loving mercy and walking humbly" they are experiencing a new power and purpose in their walk with God and people.

WHAT IS STOPPING US?

God calls the church to be both a prophetic voice and a demonstration of His commitment to justice for the poor and disenfranchised. If the early church joyfully embraced this call, what is it that keeps the church in our time from actively pursuing justice? What are the barriers that have gotten in the way? Many believers have much too small a vision of the extent, power and immediacy of the Kingdom of God. The issue of global poverty, even poverty in our own town, seems too big to tackle, yet the Kingdom is big enough and powerful enough to bring about fundamental change wherever it comes. If we see the gospel of the Kingdom as limited to salvation and even healing, then our understanding is too small. The gospel that says essentially, "Come to Jesus, wait for heaven, and I will see you there," is not good news to the poor.

The priorities and methodologies of the Western church are all too often difficult to differentiate from those of the world. How much thought and money go into many churches' strategies for attracting people? Jesus called the church to be counter-cultural, and where the church has flourished, it has always stood in contrast to the culture around it. The first beatitude in the Sermon on the Mount declared blessing on the poor in spirit; in Luke's version of the Sermon, blessing was declared upon those who are simply poor. Jesus was saying that in spite of your poverty, not because of it, the blessings of the Kingdom come to you. Jesus declared a revolutionary gospel, pronouncing a whole new order. He turns everything upside down and this is why He was persecuted and ultimately executed. Whenever the church fully committed itself to the gospel that Jesus proclaimed, it found itself in direct conflict with the culture surrounding it and the Powers That Be that control that culture. The enemy of the gospel is the teaching that we are to be a success, that it is the winners who enjoy God's blessing. So much of our preaching and our books direct the church on how to be a success in the world. Even the money and the energy that we put into creating impressive buildings and programs reveal our desire to look attractive and successful.

Related to this issue of an ethic of success is the reality that our money insulates us from the lifestyle of the poor. We do not have to live among them; even in our own towns and cities we often do not frequent the same stores and restaurants. The truly poor are rarely found in restaurants. Our money also isolates us from their experience. This is especially true with the poor overseas. We know very little about their struggle to survive, and when we become aware of it, our money makes it much easier to simply write a check than to get directly involved in helping them. This is why I believe that Christians in the West need to set aside both the time and the finances to go and encounter our brothers and sisters in the developing world. Too often, as I have invited men and women that come with me to the front lines, I have heard, "It's just not convenient for me right now." Jesus never, ever called us to a lifestyle of convenience and preference. This is the value of the world around us, a value that is increasingly infiltrating the church.

Whether or not we will engage in the cause of justice and bringing help and hope revolves around two words – today and soon. God's word is "Today." *"Today, if you hear His voice, do not harden your hearts"* (Heb. 4:7). Paul wrote to the Corinthians, *"Now is the favorable time; behold, now is the day of salvation"* (2 Cor. 6:2 ESV). After Jesus stood up in the synagogue and read from the scroll of Isaiah, He said, *"Today this scripture has been fulfilled in your hearing"* (Luke 4:21). There is always a sense of immediacy in following Jesus. In the gospels Jesus' invitation always required an immediate choice; He never tried to persuade or manipulate, He simply invited them to come and follow Him now. Like the disciples, we have a decision to make and as Billy Graham has famously said, "To not decide is a decision."

I think that our adversary, the one who wants to stop the purposes of God from being released upon the earth, the one against whom the Kingdom of God is advancing – this one has a word as well. It is "Soon." As long as we let our hearts get a little bit stirred but are not actually activated, our adversary wins. We can do more and do it quicker than we ever imagined, but we must do something. "Today" makes John 1:14 a daily reality in our lives and releases all the potential that is waiting for us in the Kingdom. "Soon" is not only an excuse, it is not only another way to insulate ourselves from the issue of injustice and the plight of the poor, but "soon" perpetually keeps us from the great adventure of being disciples of Jesus.

THE JUSTICE ACTIVATING QUESTION: WHO IS MY NEIGHBOR?

Jesus told us that all of the Law and the Prophets can be summed up in one command: Love God with all that you have and love your neighbor as yourself. Confronted with this truth, one of His listeners tried to evade the responsibility of this command by asking, *"Who is my neighbor?"* Jesus told the story that connected living rightly (Mic. 6:8) with an understanding of who our neighbor really is. This story, in Luke 10, is one of learning to see those who were once invisible to us, the ones on the side of the road. It is a story meant to provoke us to stop and do something. Jesus puts the one on the side of the road in front of us because He knows that we can be His hands and feet at a critical moment in that person's life. Previously, I wrote that the narrowness of the Jericho Road makes this story one about awareness; we cannot avoid the one on the side of the road. This is also a story of activated mercy and justice.

For the past several years Impact Nations has been going to Payatas, a garbage dump in Manila where over one hundred thousand people live. One of the most limited resources in Payatas is medical care, so we have gone once or twice each year to conduct mobile medical clinics. During one of these, a community member thanked me for conducting the clinic. I replied truthfully that it was our privilege and we were glad to be a small help. As he looked out over the hundreds of children with their mothers who were waiting for care, he said, "I don't think you understand the significance of this clinic. In this community the people know that their lives are not valued by others. They know they cannot get medical care and so when their children become ill, they keep them indoors and let the sickness run its course, not knowing whether their child will live or die. You see all these mothers with their children? You have given them hope today. That is why they have come." God values the poor and He wants them cared for with dignity.

A short while later a crisis arose at the clinic. Three children who were extremely sick were brought to our medical director. Some of the sickest children that we see anywhere in the world are living in this garbage dump. Our medical director was sure that these children had bacterial meningitis, which is deadly and highly contagious. I remember the sight of the smallest one being held in a team member's arms, unconscious with her eyes rolled back. A minute or two later, her older sister went into convulsions. It turns out that all three of them were being raised by their grandmother because the parents had deserted the children. In her one room shack there were five children sleeping in one bed. A couple of the team members laid hands on the children and commanded the sickness to go in Jesus' name. We then had a team member drive these children to the nearest hospital.

Then things got even more interesting. When the grandmother discovered that we were taking the children to the hospital for emergency treatment she became angry, in fact enraged. This precipitated a discussion back and forth for several minutes. We could not understand why she was upset, and she could not understand why we would take those kids to the hospital. Finally her concern became clear to us when through the translator she said, "You have ruined me. I will never be able to pay the hospital back for this treatment. What have you done to me?" Our medical director was shocked and said to her, "Mama, we will pay for the treatment. Of course we will pay." In the economic inequity of our two cultures, what was a ruinous and insurmountable amount to this woman was actually a very small amount for us.

At the hospital, the team member waited with these desperately sick children … and waited. This was not because there were many serious emergencies ahead of her; it was simply because these poor and dirty children were of no value. Finally, she went to the intake desk and demanded that these children be seen. We need to stand up for the rights of the weak and the poor. This is standing in the gap. But now something amazing happened. The children were carried in to see a doctor, and at that moment the healing power of God touched their bodies. The fevers immediately left, the baby became conscious, and the girl stopped convulsing.

The final scene of this story took place that night when, as this community now gathered to sing and to hear the good news of the gospel and to receive healing prayer for everyone, the little girl who that afternoon had been sick almost to the point of death was now running and dancing. Meanwhile, her grandmother, smiling broadly, held the now healthy toddler on her knee. When the Kingdom comes, everything changes. What was impossible is now possible. The Kingdom comes with justice – the restoration of the life that God always intended.

The answer to the question, "Who is my neighbor?" is changing in our day. The answer is getting bigger, more all-encompassing. It is also becoming more immediate. With modern communication, the internet, social networks and instant money transfers to anywhere in the world, the Jericho road has become a global highway. However, the intent of Jesus' answer has remained the same. If we will follow Him, we will carry His love of mercy and His passion for justice. If we do otherwise, we are without excuse. Grace and truth are what Jesus gives us. God confronts us, the Church, with His truth, and like Jesus' story to the lawyer who was looking for a loophole, there is no wiggle room:

> *If you fail under pressure,*
> *your strength is too small.*
> *Rescue those who are unjustly sentenced to die;*
> *save them as they stagger to their death.*
> *Don't excuse yourself by saying, "Look, we didn't know."*
> *For God understands all hearts, and he sees you.*
> *He who guards your soul knows you knew.*
> *He will repay all people as their actions deserve.*
> (Prov. 24:10–12 NLT)

More than at any other time, the church in the West is accountable for what it knows. We cannot say that we are overcommitted elsewhere. We cannot say that we would like to do more, but it is simply not in our budget. We cannot say that this does not fit with our mission statement. In 2011 the evening news was full of coverage of the famine and genocide going on in Somalia. The Dadaab refugee camp in Kenya, seventy miles from Somalia, was in my living room every night. This is the camp that I went to in 2005 when there were 136,000 refugees; now there are over a half million with fifteen thousand being added weekly.

The needs, of course, have never been greater, but likewise neither have the opportunities. I believe that the Spirit of God has been moving powerfully over the last several years regarding this issue of justice. Those outside the church have become much more aware of global poverty and many of them are asking what can be done. I believe God is speaking through the music and the movies of our age. It is very interesting to see how many Hollywood actors are leveraging their fame in order to bring awareness of the plight of the poor in places like Africa and Haiti. As He has so often done throughout history, God is raising up prophetic voices from very surprising places – a number of them outside the church. One of these prophetic voices is Bono, who is using his fame, influence and wealth to awaken the west to the plight of the poor in Africa. Addressing an audience in Washington DC, Bono said,

"So you've been doing God's work, but what's God working on now? What's God working on this year? Two and a half million Africans are going to die of AIDS. What's God working on now? I meet the people who tell me it's going to take an act of God to stop this plague. Well, I don't believe that. I think God is waiting for us to act … Waiting for us to recognize that distance can no longer decide who is our neighbor. We can't choose our neighbors anymore. We can't choose the benefits of globalization without some of the responsibilities and we should remind ourselves that "love thy neighbor" is not advice: it is a command."[21]

Today over sixteen thousand people will be infected with HIV;

---

21 <http://www.atu2.com/news/africares-annual-bishop-walker-awards-dinner-washington-dc.html>.

another eight thousand will die today because of AIDS. In Uganda ninety percent of those infected with HIV this year will be women, most of them because of rape. This pandemic, perhaps more than anything in all of history, daily highlights the impact of injustice upon the poor. For this disease moves through the arenas of gender inequality, educational opportunity and geography. As Bono says, "Where you live should not decide whether you live or whether you die." One of the greatest ways to fight this plague is through education. When children have at least a Grade Six education their chance of contracting HIV falls by fifty percent; with a high school education it falls by eighty-five percent. A young actress friend of mine went to Africa in order to use her skills to teach about HIV/ AIDS prevention and sexual health in remote villages. As I write this, I have another friend in Central America right now doing the same. Every disciple has something to offer; every follower of Jesus can make a difference and rescue lives.

From cover to cover God's Word to His people is to pursue justice on behalf of the disadvantaged.

> *"If you will swear by My name alone, and begin to live good, honest lives and uphold justice, then you will be a blessing to the nations of the world, and all people will come and praise My name"* (Jer. 4:2 NLT).

All the way back in Genesis 12:1–3 God made a remarkable promise to his friend Abraham. God told Abraham that He would bless him, that He would bless his descendants, and through them He would bless all the people groups of the earth. Jeremiah tells us that justice releases God's covenant with Abraham; as we pursue justice all people will be blessed. This verse sends us to the nations with a God-given mandate. It also commissions us to receive, include and actively interact with people from around the world. Furthermore, as we uphold justice people see God for who He really is: *"The Lord, the Lord, the compassionate and gracious God, slow to anger, abounding in love and faithfulness, maintaining love to thousands, and forgiving wickedness, rebellion and sin"* (Exod. 34:6–7).

As the nations discover the God of mercy and justice, He receives the glory due His Name.

"Let the nations be glad and sing for joy, for you judge the peoples with equity and guide the nations upon earth" (Psa. 67:4 ESV).

AN INESCAPABLE TRUTH

In Matthew's gospel account, Jesus' final public teaching presents a truth of ultimate consequence. It is at once marvelous and terrifying in its implications.

When the Son of Man comes in His glory, and all the angels with Him, then He will sit on His glorious throne. All the nations will be gathered before Him; and He will separate them from one another, as the shepherd separates the sheep from the goats; and He will set the sheep on His right, and the goats on the left. Then the King will say to those on His right, 'Come, you who are blessed of My Father, inherit the kingdom prepared for you from the foundation of the world. For I was hungry, and you gave Me something to eat; I was thirsty, and you gave Me something to drink; I was a stranger, and you invited Me in; naked, and you clothed Me; I was sick, and you visited Me; I was in prison and you came to Me.'

Then the righteous will answer Him, 'Lord, when did we see You hungry, and feed You, or thirsty, and give You something to drink? When did we see You a stranger, and invite You in, or naked, and clothe You? When did we see You sick, or in prison, and come to You?' The King will answer and say to them, 'Truly I say to you, to the extent

that you did it to one of these brothers of Mine, even the
least of these them, you did it to Me" (Matt. 25:31–40
NLT).

Jesus unveiled what was to happen before God's judgment seat,
what the Old Testament referred to as "the Day of the Lord." This
is perhaps the clearest picture in all of scripture of the contrasting
fate of those who are welcomed by the Lord and those who are
not. Jesus reveals that our decisions have consequences. Ironically,
at this throne of judgment, our decisions are finished – now it is
time for the King to decide, and His decisions determine eternal
destinies.

One the most striking features of these words is that it is not
ministry on a grand scale that captures Jesus' notice; what He
weighs is our interactions with "one of the least." Jesus' emphasis
on the lowly individual should encourage us greatly; in a world
filled with needs that can overwhelm us, Jesus is saying that what
we do with needy individuals is what matters in His Kingdom.
That is why the magnitude of the needs can never exempt us from
caring for the one He puts in front of us. Real change, authentic
rescue, happens one small person at a time.

Who are the "least of these brothers [and sisters] of Mine"?
The universal setting of all nations and every person, the universal
suffering of hunger, thirst, loneliness, nakedness, sickness and
imprisonment all indicate that Jesus is referring to how the life
of everyone in every nation will be judged according to how they
responded to the hurting and needy around them – not just limited
to other believers. These words teach us that our love for others
cannot be selective. The faithful church that follows the way of
Jesus cannot limit itself to good works within the church. Jesus'
arms have always been much too wide for that.

Jesus surprises His disciples and us when He says that caring
for the least of these is not as though we are caring for Him, it
is actually caring for Him. We are immediately struck with the

implications: first, we encounter Jesus all the time in the midst of poverty and injustice, and likely do not recognize Him; secondly, every person, in every nation has access to Jesus through a needy, hurting person. Frederick Bruner proposes that those who have never heard the gospel or received Christ will be judged on the Day of the Lord by how they received Jesus in others.[22] This should not surprise us. After all, in the fifth Beatitude, Jesus promised: *"Blessed are the merciful, for they will be shown mercy"* (Matt. 5:7). Indeed, the culmination of all history reveals the remarkable mercy of our Lord.

BUT OUR MERCIFUL LORD IS ALSO A GOD OF HOLY LOVE

Then the King will turn to those on the left and say, "Away with you, you cursed ones, into the eternal fire prepared for the devil and his demons. For I was hungry, and you didn't feed me. I was thirsty, and you didn't give me a drink. I was a stranger, and you didn't invite me into your home. I was naked, and you didn't give me clothing. I was sick and in prison, and you didn't visit me" (Matt. 25:41–43 NLT).

These are perhaps Jesus' strongest words of judgment; their sheer awfulness and finality, when honestly faced, drive us to repent for our lack of mercy and compassion, and for our failure to fight injustice on behalf of the least. We cannot be selective in who we will love. Neither can we ignore Jesus' words to the religious leaders, *"I desire mercy and not sacrifice"* (Matt. 9:13). Clearly, what matters to the Lord is not our religious service, but that we are faithful to ministering to Jesus as we encounter Him in the lives of the poor and oppressed. There is simply no way around this. Martin Luther wrote:

---

22 Frederick D. Bruner, *The Churchbook Matthew 13–28* (Grand Rapids: Eerdmans, 2007), 572.

Oh dear Lord God! How are we so blind that we don't take such love to heart! Who could have thought it up that God Himself throws Himself so deep down into our midst and accepts the works of all those who give themselves to the poor as though they were done for Him. Thus the world is full, full of God – in every alley, before your door, you find Christ.[23]

In both Luke and Matthew's account, Jesus praises and rebukes not only individuals, but entire communities according to how they have responded to Him (Matt. 11:20–24; Luke 10:13–15). It is also interesting that in Matthew 25, there is a gathering of the nations; the Day of the Lord speaks of not only individual, but corporate accountability.

Jesus told us that whoever seeks to hold onto his life on his own terms, will lose his life; however, the great paradox is that when we give up life on our own terms, we will find true life. I am convinced that this word is not merely for individuals, but for Christ's bride, His church. We live in an enigmatic time: never has there been such an ability to effect real and almost immediate change among the least of our brothers and sisters; yet, there has never been as much pressure on the Western church to conform to the values of success and prestige as at this time in history. This is why over the past thirty years, the percentage of church budgets that go to overseas missions and the poor have steadily dropped as well-meaning leaders have succumbed to the pressure to have bigger, newer buildings and to provide more and more programs requiring a steadily increasing number of full time paid staff. The average number of staff among large North American churches has increased by fifty percent in nine years. Sixty-two cents from every budget dollar goes to payroll and facilities, while only two cents goes to missions.

---

23 Martin Luther, *Sammtliche Schriften* (2nd ed; St Louis 1880, ed. J.G.Walch). Cited in F.D. Bruner, *Ibid*, 582.

In our churches, we have embraced a worldview of competitiveness, material success and comfort. There is great pressure on pastors and leaders to have the best musicians, children's programs, facilities and staff. Otherwise, the church faces decline as members go to those churches that provide these. Not bad people, but a bad system that does not embrace the truth of losing our lives for the sake of the gospel

Jesus said that we cannot serve God and Gain (mammon), even when it looks like Gain will help us to serve God. And when the church falls into this, Jesus – in the guise of the poor, the outcast, the oppressed – suffers. In trying to save its life, the church loses its call to participate with Jesus in His great Kingdom cause of bringing the reality of heaven to earth with all of its restoring and rescuing power. This is a call of eternal and ultimate significance. We, the church, enter into this adventure in only one way – losing our lives with their preferences and priorities, and embracing the values of our King.

The apostle Paul wrote to the church in Corinth, reminding them that on that day, the Lord will weigh the value of what they have built according to His standard.

> *But each one should be careful how he builds. For no one can lay any foundation other than the one already laid, which is Jesus Christ. If any man builds on this foundation using gold, silver, costly stones, wood, hay or straw, his work will be shown for what it is, because the Day will bring it to light. It will be revealed with fire, and the fire will test the quality of each man's work. If what he has built survives, he will receive his reward. If it is burned up, he will suffer loss; he himself will be saved, but only as one escaping through the flames* (1 Cor. 3:10–15).

With all my heart I believe that, as we will surely give an account for our priorities and values, revealed and defined by our expenditures and efforts, the 21st century church will face a great reckoning.

Isaiah 28:17 tells us that God evaluates what we have built by one standard: justice and righteousness. In Matthew 25, Jesus has brought us face to face with the nature and the eternal consequences of that final evaluation. He is telling us that it is not in the great activities, not in the major strategies, not in the obvious successes where Jesus is found; no, Jesus so identifies with the hungry, the captive, the poor and the oppressed, that if we will really care for Him, we must do so through the least of His brothers and sisters. As with most things in the Kingdom of God, the way up is the way down; the only way to gain what is ultimately real, is to lose what we now hold in our hands. If we will make the exchange, like the merchant who sold everything that he had relied upon, we will find ourselves with the pearl that Jesus always intended for His church.

Love and faithfulness meet together;
righteousness and peace kiss each other.
Faithfulness springs forth from the earth,
and righteousness looks down from heaven.
The LORD will indeed give what is good,
and our land will yield its harvest.
Righteousness goes before him
and prepares the way for his steps.
(Psa. 85:10–13)

13

VUKANI:
A CALL TO ACTION

And the Word became flesh; the ideal became real.
JOHN 1:14
E. Stanley Jones paraphrase

Vukani: a Zulu word meaning, "Get up and do something."

The gospel accounts provide us with an interesting snapshot of how Jesus called disciples to follow Him. He did not say, "Follow Me, and I will lead you to the Father; I will heal the brokenness in your hearts and lives." Clearly, these great blessings did change their lives forever, but they were not the focus of His invitation. Instead, Jesus invited the disciples into purpose. "I will make you fishers of men – there is a job to do!" His call is an invitation into His great cause: the rescue of men, women and children, the restoration of life as God always intended it to be. As we have seen, this rescue mission involves *all* the signs of the coming of God's Kingdom to earth – the sick and injured are healed; people's hearts are changed and they are brought into a whole new Christ-imbued life; God's justice transforms individuals and entire communities.

Jesus' invitation has never changed. When we responded to Him, we came for ourselves. Our eyes were opened to our need for a savior, a rescuer to wash our hearts clean and to bring us to the Father. Without this amazing work of His grace and power, we have no hope. However, like Isaiah, Jesus calls us to: *"Lift up your*

205

eyes to the heavens, And look on the earth beneath" (Isa. 51:6 NKJV).

In His exchange with the disciples outside the Samaritan village (John 4), Jesus exhorted them to lift up their eyes – to get a higher perspective of God's activities. He also told them to eliminate excuses. "Do not say, 'Four more months till the harvest.'" Jesus was acutely aware of the almost universal tendency to delay, especially when we do not perceive the activity of heaven and the cosmic stakes involved. Today, He would tell us not to think that we are not yet ready, that if we just had a bit more training, if we attended another couple of conferences or read another Christian book, *then* we would be ready to step out.

As Isaiah, Daniel, Ezekiel, John and so many others saw, the Kingdom of God is accelerating in its advancement. I spoke with someone about a man in India who came to Christ only four years ago and has now seen twenty-three thousand new believers baptized. The church is growing all over the developing world at a rate that would have been almost unimaginable twenty-five years ago. Jesus, looking ahead to this time in history, said: *"And this gospel of the kingdom will be preached in all the world as a witness to all the nations, and then the end will come"* (Matt. 24:14 NKJV).

This is the greatest call of all – to participate with God in His ultimate purpose. We were made for this. For all who have the Spirit of Christ beating inside them, moving in the rhythm of His Kingdom awakens the deepest places of our being. How often I have heard men and women say as they have followed Jesus into the midst of what He is doing, "I was made for this!" And indeed we were.

Everything hinges on making a decision: to step out of our comfort and over our fears in order to follow the One who continues to say, "Come." Jesus said that if we are going to be His disciples, then we have to follow Him to where He is going. And He is on the move. When He walked the earth, Jesus' food was to do the will and works of the Father (John 4:34). This is His invitation to disciples. Saying 'yes' moves us from the ideal to the real, from being conceptual to active followers.

Moving in the rhythm of the Kingdom requires constant choices. As we choose to be available for Kingdom activity, we soon discover that Jesus really *does* ask us to embrace new values and priorities. This will often change the way we spend our time (even our vacations!), our money and our willingness to live risky and compassionate lives. Giving our lives to Christ may begin with a heart-felt decision at the altar to receive His wonderful gift of eternal life; however, the transition from believer to disciple means quite literally "giving Him our lives." If my life is His, then I have lost control over it. But here is the great paradox of the Kingdom: *"Whoever loses his life for My sake, will* find *it"* (Matt 16:25 ESV). This is the great promise, both the joy and the power of the gospel. This is the abundant, purposeful life that Jesus shares with those who walk the disciple's road with Him.

At the heart of every true disciple's journey with Jesus is *trust*. It is not belief in the existence of God or the truth of the gospel, but *trust* that is the great watershed. It takes trust to follow Jesus into uncertainty and instability; and it is only when we step out upon this journey that trust can grow. For a great many twenty-first century Christians, seeking clarity and security regarding the future is so highly valued that life is structured in order to minimize the risk of having to trust God. This is why Jesus insisted that disciples refuse to worry.

> *Don't worry and ask yourselves, 'Will we have anything to eat? Will we have anything to drink? Will we have any clothes to wear?' Only people who don't know God are always worrying about such things. Your Father in heaven knows that you need all of these. But more than anything else, put God's work first and do what he wants. Then the other things will be yours as well* (Matt. 6:31–33 CEV).

Jesus knows that worry neutralizes and paralyzes us, destroying the childlike trust that is the foundation of our relationship with Him and the Father. That is why trusting Him was not a suggestion, but a command: *"Do not let your hearts be troubled. Trust in God; trust also in Me"* (John 14:1).

Brennan Manning has written in *Ruthless Trust*:

> The basic premise of biblical trust is the conviction that God wants us to grow, to unfold, and to experience fullness of life. However, this kind of trust is acquired only gradually and most often through a series of crises and trials.[24]

Trust requires a willingness to embrace a Father who desires and has planned good things for us – not necessarily easy things, but significant things, activities through which we participate in His great cosmic plan. Perhaps even more so, trust requires a willingness to look beyond our own failures, inconsistencies and weakness to the person that Christ sees when He calls us from the other side of the cross. From His eternal perspective, Jesus sees all that we can be; in fact, all that we *will* be, if we will keep our eyes on Him and not on ourselves.

Disciples are those who have crossed this threshold of trust. They have seen a more eternal and vital vision and have said "yes" to it. Disciples have put their hand to the plow and refused to look back (Luke 9:62). They have counted the cost of following Jesus and discovered a return on the investment of their lives of thirty, sixty and a hundred fold. These are the men and women through whom Christ and His Kingdom move, bringing the hope and change for which the world longs.

Over the years I have had the opportunity to know and observe many of these men and women, in both the western world and

---

24 Brennan Manning, *Ruthless Trust* (New York: HarperCollins, 2000), 9.

developing nations. Most of them work quietly, below the radar of the world's attention. But like the seed, salt and yeast about which Jesus spoke, the Kingdom of God slowly and steadily advances through the work of their lives.

A single, middle-aged North American woman who has worked for most of her life in a low paying job, hears about AIDS orphans in Zambia without homes. In response, she sells her modest home, buys a smaller one, and uses the remaining money to build an orphanage. A college professor in India abandons financial security and a great career in order to lay down her life for the poor. Day after day, year after year she goes out to *live* the compassion and sacrifice of Christ for the desperate. A successful young businessman takes all that he has saved and begins a business in an African nation that will provide employment and training; the profits are used to feed orphans.

None of these would say that they have sacrificed. Certainly, they see nothing heroic in their actions and if this was pointed out to them, their response would likely be, *"We are unworthy servants; we have only done our duty"* (Luke 17:10). Yet a sense of duty is not what motivates them. Rather, they have discovered the abandoned, purposeful life of a disciple; and over the joy of having discovered this great treasure they gladly gave up their old lives in order to possess something greater (Matt. 13:44).

There is something deeply heroic about disciples – not the bluster of "living large" that the world so readily identifies, but the steady, unwavering lives of those who have heard and embraced Jesus' invitation to follow Him, no matter where He is going. These kinds of disciples come with a great variety of gifts, callings and personalities, yet they have some foundational qualities in common.

DISCIPLES HAVE A STRONG VISION

They allow themselves to dream big dreams. The apostle Paul said this to the Ephesians: *"Now all glory to God, who is able, through his mighty power at work within us, to accomplish infinitely more than we might ask or think"* (Eph. 3:20 NLT). One translation says "beyond our wildest dreams." God's dreams for us are big dreams. Of course, He is the creator of everything, He is limitless, and He has a great cosmic plan and invites us to be participants. C. S. Lewis wrote, "If we consider the unblushing promises of reward and the staggering nature of the rewards promised in the Gospels, it would seem that Our Lord finds our desires not too strong, but too weak."[25]

These men and women recognize the power of vision both in their own lives and those around them. They are forward-looking; they can see a better future, and they can see it as if it were present. This simply reflects the heart of their Creator who *"calls forth the things that are not as though they were"* (Rom. 4:17). The apostle Paul understood the power of vision in his life:

> *I am focusing all my energies on this one thing: Forgetting the past and looking forward to what lies ahead, I strain to reach the end of the race and receive the prize for which God, through Christ Jesus, is calling us up to heaven* (Phil. 3:13–14 TLB).

Vision provides powerful protection from discouragement, fear and distraction. Proverbs 29:18 tells us, *"Where there is no vision, the people perish."* Vision directs our steps and enables us to order our priorities. Conversely, lack of vision attracts our enemy, and he comes with depression, confusion, even sickness.

DISCIPLES LIVE WITH A STRONG SENSE OF PURPOSE

In his remarkable letter to the Ephesians, the apostle Paul wrote,

---

25 C.S. Lewis, *The Weight of Glory* (New York: HarperCollins 1949), 26.

"In him we were also chosen, having been predestined according to the plan of him who works out everything in conformity with the purpose of his will" (Eph. 1:11).

The New Testament writers were constantly calling the church up to a greater awareness of the identity and authority that they had because of their relationship with Christ. Paul is reminding his readers that from the beginning of time, God has set them apart; He has chosen them with a pre-determined plan. The word "predestined" is packed with meaning, including "to have a horizon set." God has placed a specific horizon in front of every believer. He has a specific destiny for them that is not so much a guarantee, as an invitation. It is as though He is saying to us, "Look through My eyes and see what I see for your life. And look at how far-reaching is My plan for you." Disciples live deliberately, knowing that their sense of purpose is what propels them to the horizon that God has set before them.

King David is a wonderful example of a life lived with purpose and focus. *"I cry out to God Most High, to God, who fulfills his purpose for me"* (Psa. 57:2). David was confident in God's unique purpose for his life. In the midst of adversity, disappointment and challenge, this empowered him to live with single-mindedness. Disciples live with confidence that God delights to reveal His assignment to His children. They pay attention to the dreams and visions that God is putting in their heart, understanding that those are like stepping-stones that reveal God's destiny for them. They have a strong sense that nothing is ever wasted, whether or not they understand in the short term the purpose for each step along the way.

As disciples move in the center of God's call for them, they experience the acceleration and expansion of favor. One of the ways that we can know we are in the center of God's assignment for our lives is that we are surrounded by favor. This is because it requires supernatural favor to accomplish the assignment. Because

I am in the bull's-eye of my assignment, I find myself meeting with governors, cabinet ministers and national leaders in the developing world. At home, I do not often connect with such people of power and influence because I do not need to in order to fulfill God's assignment; but overseas, God continually surprises me with the doors that He opens.

Solomon exhorts us to live our lives with focus: *"Look straight ahead, and fix your eyes on what lies before you. Mark out a straight path for your feet; then stick to the path and stay safe. Don't get sidetracked"* (Prov. 4:25–27 NLT). Living intentionally is key to living like David, watching God fulfill His purpose for our lives. It also protects us from the disempowerment of distraction.

DISCIPLES LIVE WITH PASSION

I am not referring to fiery personalities; some of the heroic men and women I have the privilege to know have very quiet demeanors. Rather, there is an internal fire that never seems to go out and always propels disciples forward. It takes passion to break free from the status quo. It takes passion to say "no" to the voices around us that continuously try to tame our vision.

I grew up in the era of the Mercury, Gemini and Apollo space programs. I well remember gathering in the gymnasium to watch a blurry image of John Glenn lifting off from Cape Canaveral (to tell the truth, the most exciting part for me was getting out of Math class!). Many of us remember the enormous Saturn V rockets that lifted the space capsules off the launch pad. They were so large because they had to break through the gravitational pull of the Earth. The rockets strained to climb vertically but after a few minutes they lifted the capsule beyond the pull of gravity. After that it was clear sailing – not without challenges and dangers, but no longer wrestling against the restrictive pull of gravity. The passion that the disciple carries in his heart is very much like that Saturn V rocket. It takes passion to break away from the pull of things like security, success, being affirmed and being understood by friends and family members. That is why Jesus told his listeners that if they would follow Him it would cost them what the world says is precious. But once that decision is made and begins to be walked out, the pull of the status quo steadily diminishes and a new freedom comes. *"So Christ has truly set us free. Now make sure that you stay free"* (Gal. 5:1 NLT). *So If the Son sets you free, you are truly free"* (John 8:36 NLT).

The challenges differ from place to place and generation to generation, but it has always taken passion to blaze a new trail. A great hero of the faith is William Carey. God gave him a vision to reach India at a time when there were no missionaries there. He was consistently resisted but the fire in him propelled his vision forward. When no missionary society would accept him, Carey began his own society. His vision was costly: he lost two wives and several children, close friends and coworkers died; he was even expelled from his own missionary society but he never quit. This hero worked tirelessly for years, passionately committed to seeing the gospel proclaimed and received throughout India. In his lifetime Carey saw very few converts but he was blazing a trail for thousands to follow. I suppose that Carey's life and sacrifice has touched me so deeply because of my love for India and because the trail he blazed has now led to over one hundred fifty million Indians coming into the Kingdom of God. When I stand in a village and preach the gospel, sometimes to people who have never heard the name of Jesus, and I see so many healed and come to a saving faith, I cannot help but think of the passion and fire of William Carey and what a great debt we owe.

DISCIPLES CREATE AND RESTORE

Let us make people in our image, to be like ourselves. They will be masters over all life (Gen. 1:26 NLT).

We are made in the image of the God of infinite creativity. God is always creating because that is who He is; it is His essence to create. That's why the universe is continually expanding. How could a finite universe reflect the infinite creativity of God? I am always amazed at the creative ideas and solutions that come from disciples. That is why my role is largely to provide opportunities for others and then get out of the way. As a result, there is always a multiplication of ministry. The example the disciple's life gives, inspires others to likewise abandon themselves to a similar lifestyle of following Jesus wherever He is going. When it comes to extending the Kingdom of God, I find it interesting that Jesus told us *what* to do, but He did not tell us exactly *how* to do it. Because they are so focused and confident about God's purpose in their lives, disciples can be especially flexible and creative in how to fulfill that purpose.

"Now we look inside, and what we see is that anyone united with the Messiah gets a fresh start, is created new. The old life is gone; a new life burgeons!" (2 Cor. 5:17 MSG). This verse reflects the heart of creativity and restoration. Every time disciples see men and women give their lives to Jesus or have their bodies healed of pain and sickness, disciples are deeply aware that they are engaged in the Family Business.

There is a sense of urgency in disciples. They recognize that, by its very nature, the process of restoration and creating new possibilities continues to propel them forward. With every encounter, disciples expect the reality of heaven to come and touch people and situations; they expect God to use them to restore lives. When the sick are healed and the deaf hear, when the hungry are fed, when the oppressed and outcast are given hope – then the Kingdom has come. Disciples participate in the creative, restorative activity of God. This is why disciples can never accept the status quo. Because they are following Jesus in radical obedience, they are compelled to push against inertia, apathy and acceptance of things, as "that's just the way it is." As we have established earlier, the Kingdom of God is the power of heaven coming to earth. It is a creative and restorative power. That is at the heart of the Family Business; disciples who live heroically are fully committed to this business.

DISCIPLES UPHOLD JUSTICE

I have already written about justice in previous chapters, so let me just express this: It is impossible for disciples – for those who follow Jesus as he runs into the darkness – it is impossible for them to ignore injustice. When they see injustice, their hearts are deeply moved with both compassion and holy anger. This compels them to take action, to "stand in the gap." When justice, the restoration of life as God intended it to be, comes to a person, family or village, it brings great joy to their hearts. They understand that the issue of justice is central to the heart of a disciple, just as it is central to the heart of Jesus.

DISCIPLES PERSEVERE

Ralph Waldo Emerson once wrote,

> The characteristic of genuine heroism is its persistency. All men have wandering impulses, fits and starts of generosity. But when you have resolved to be great, abide by yourself, and do not weakly try to reconcile yourself with the world. The heroic cannot be the common, nor the common the heroic. [26]

It takes courage, conviction, passion and stamina in order to persevere. While Emerson was describing "world-shakers," the

---

26 The Selected Writings of Ralph Waldo Emerson <http://philosophersnotes.com/quotes/by_topic/Hero/page/2>.

same can be said about the perseverance of disciples. Their heroic exploits are not likely seen by the world, but Hebrews tells us that heaven sees and cheers them on.

The Message translates the beginning of Hebrews 12 with great vibrancy:

> *Do you see what this means – all these pioneers who blazed the way, all these veterans cheering us on? It means we'd better get on with it. Strip down, start running – and never quit! No extra spiritual fat, no parasitic sins. Keep your eyes on Jesus, who both began and finished this race we're in. Study how he did it. Because he never lost sight of where he was headed – that exhilarating finish in and with God – he could put up with anything along the way: cross, shame, whatever* (Heb. 12:1–2).

When tempted to give in to fear or discouragement and quit, the Bible encourages us to focus on the example of Jesus. And more than being inspired, we can draw upon His life beating inside of us. In an era of instant gratification and seeking short-term results, the endurance and perseverance of disciples mark them as a different kind of person: counter-cultural salt and light in a world desperately in need.

DISCIPLES TAKE RISKS

This may be the most distinct characteristic of a disciple. From the beginning, following Jesus meant risk-taking. From the very moment when disciples responded to His invitation to follow Him, they were stepping into a world of uncertainty and risk. Risk-taking is the very lifestyle of disciples. Whatever level of change, whatever step of obedience that disciples take, they are moving from the known to the unknown. This is the arena where we must trust Jesus. To say that we trust Him and yet refuse to take risks is a contradiction in terms. This may be the clearest dividing line between believers who are saved by grace and are going to heaven, and disciples who follow Jesus into the rescue mission. To read the gospels, to read the letters written to the early church, and to read the book of Revelation is to come face to face with the reality of the first cost of discipleship. Jesus is calling us to set aside our sense of security and certainty, and step into the unknown and the unsure. I agree with Bono who has said, "This is no burden; this is a great adventure." But it is an adventure that cannot even be started without the willingness to take risks. Jesus told Peter and the other disciples that following Him would cost them everything – house, proximity to family, capital "lands," job security and reputation. Yet in the same breath He said that we would receive many times more. In Mark, the earliest Gospel, Jesus says we will receive them in this life.

Taking risks for the sake of the gospel and for Jesus always takes us through a tight place. There is a great testing that comes. The essence of this test has never changed from the beginning of the Bible. We are always challenged with the question, "Did God really say?" It is in the arena of risk that God forms us and prepares us for His great purposes in our lives. The only people who think that these tight places, these testing times are exciting are those who have never been through them. They are designed to refine us.

Jesus usually begins by inviting us to take relatively small risks – perhaps go on a short-term mission trip, or give some disposable income to someone in need. Maybe He invites us to ask a stranger for the first time, "May I pray for you?". Whatever it is, when we step over our discomfort in order to say yes, the Kingdom begins to grow in us and we have begun the journey of discipleship. As we continue to say yes, the risks increase. I think that Jesus loves to take us to the place where He must show up, where we are not able to complete the assignment on our own strength, no matter how hard we try. This of course results in our pressing into Him. He delights in this because, more than anything, He desires our hearts. So it seems that when disciples say yes to taking risks, the journey always leads them to the place of deep intimacy with Jesus, because quickly we learn that apart from Him, we can do nothing (John 15:5).

•   •   •

When the Kingdom comes, everything changes. What was impossible becomes possible. As we, like the earliest disciples, embrace this remarkable truth, our lives become instruments in the hands of Jesus Christ – instruments that He works through to bring restoration, healing and transformation. We discover that as big and all encompassing as we thought the Kingdom of God was, it is infinitely more so. The infinite and eternal King has a limitless Kingdom.

The gospel of the Kingdom is big enough and powerful enough to transform everything it touches. The gospel is so much bigger than inviting Christ into our hearts, then waiting for heaven. The gospel that Jesus and His church proclaimed and demonstrated turned the Roman world upside down. Bodies and minds were healed, lives were restored and communities were changed. The gospel has never changed.

It is a radical, risky, exhilarating message that we are invited to carry and to live. This gospel stands as a voice and demonstration of justice and righteousness; it is powerful enough to not only challenge injustice, but to break its power. This gospel embraces and follows Christ as He runs into the darkness, bringing His freedom, His remedy for the oppression, sickness and hopelessness that resides there.

This is the great cause that Christ invites us to embrace. It is bigger and more powerful than we ever dared hope; in fact, it is beyond all that we could ask or even imagine (Eph. 3:20). This is the gospel that lifts our lives into ultimate significance and purpose. It is in living this gospel that we discover the truth of His promise, that if we will lose our lives to every other cause, and embrace His cause – the Kingdom – we will find a new kind of life. It is a foretaste of the new heaven and new earth, pointing us to the great promise:

> *No eye has seen,*
> *no ear has heard,*
> *no mind has conceived*
> *what God has prepared for those who love him.*
> (1 Cor. 2:9)

So what now? How does the word become flesh, the ideal become real? Vukani. Step out and do something. Follow Jesus into an unfamiliar place. Remember, He promises to be with you as you go (Matt. 28:20). As you follow Him, as you begin to learn to move in His rhythm of empowered compassion, you will discover a supernatural favor and anointing whereby you will see more Kingdom activity happen through and around you – and see it come faster – than you ever thought possible. You and I were made for intimacy with Jesus and active participation in His Kingdom. Let this sink in: You were made for this.

How can you discover what you should do? Listen to the desires of your heart. Pay attention to what you find yourself thinking and dreaming about. Your desires will reveal your destiny. If you are unsure what your heart is telling you, then find out what God is doing and join in. Go on a short-term trip to a developing nation; join a feeding program for the poor in your city; help inner-city children to read. The list is almost endless, because God is moving in the earth. Just pick something and join in. You will find Jesus there; in fact, He has been waiting for you.

Vukani.

EPILOGUE:
THE IMPACT NATIONS STORY

"The Good News about God's kingdom will be preached in all the world, to every nation. Then the end will come."
MATTHEW 24:14 NCV

When Everything Changes reflects principles and observations that are the result of my interactions with the events and people I have encountered on my journey; therefore, it may be helpful for me to present some personal background. Being acquainted with my journey may help the reader to understand how I have arrived at some of my conclusions regarding the Kingdom of God.

"So, what do you want to do with the rest of your life? You can do anything."

I was flying somewhere over the Pacific in 2003 when these words suddenly resonated in me. I knew immediately it was God talking to me. And I knew that the answer to this question would be really important.

I had just spent two weeks in Korea. Part of that time I had been teaching a conference on marketplace ministry to Christian businessman. In one of the sessions I had asked them, "What would you do for God with the rest of your life if you could do anything and you knew that you could not fail?" It had led to the liveliest discussion of any of my sessions in the conference. Now, here I was flying back to my life in Canada as a pastor when God suddenly broke in, challenging me with the same question. I took some time to answer because I was aware of the serious implications of what I would say. After a few days I prayed, "Father, did you mean if I could do *anything?*". He answered back immediately: "Anything." Taking a deep breath, I said, "If I really can do anything with the rest of my life, I want to rescue lives. I want to rescue them spiritually, physically, economically, medically, and educationally." Even as I said these words, I felt an increase in the weightiness of His presence. Except for my wife, I told no one about this encounter. Almost immediately phone calls and e-mails started to come, many of them from people I had never heard of. Suddenly doors of invitation were opening, especially in the developing world. I was fifty years old and the direction of my life was taking a radical shift. Before very long the result was a ministry that quite literally overtook me. We called it "Impact Nations."

So how did I get there? God has created me to be a starter. Both in ministry and in my various jobs, without much exception, I found myself beginning things. Almost thirty years ago I was asked to establish two Christian schools. After a couple of years of this, I was impatient to move on to what I really wanted to do – plant churches. But the Lord kept me in schools for about five years. Although I did not realize it at the time, this experience was a large part of His preparation for me for what was coming next. My wife and I and our four boys moved three thousand miles east to plant a Vineyard church in Ontario, Canada. Ironically, we had just attended a church-planting seminar designed to help identify characteristics and traits of successful church planters. Of twenty essential traits, we discovered that we had only one! Nevertheless, God's call on us to plant a church was very strong, and so we went. In spite of our inexperience, God was very kind to us and our first church flourished wonderfully. Within just a few years we planted out from there four other churches in Ontario and, in partnership with two other Vineyard churches, a church in Russia. In 1995 my wife and I were very surprised when God called us to move to the west coast of Canada to start another Vineyard church. Once again we sold everything, packed up our children and headed west.

Over the next seven years we planted two churches in Vancouver and established a citywide House of Prayer. While pastoring, we started the Vancouver Healing Rooms, which were connected with the Healing Rooms in Spokane, Washington. From this one location the Healing Rooms steadily grew over the next four years to more than thirty communities across Canada.

These years were certainly not an unbroken series of ministry successes. God was good to us and much of what we put our hand to flourished and grew beyond our hopes. But there were also churches and ministries that struggled.

One of the things I have learned during my walk with the Lord (which began in 1976) is that with God nothing is wasted. My years in both the public and Christian school systems have taught me things that I am able to contribute now as I meet with leaders in the developing world. There was a time when I was quite intimidated by successful businessmen and indeed the whole business world. So in my journey God put me working with a multinational computer company where I rubbed elbows with businessmen every day for two years. I thought God was just providing for us as we were trying to plant our first church; but He always sees the whole picture and orders our steps accordingly. As the founder of Impact Nations, I now spend a great deal of my time with businessmen, evaluating and planning potential businesses for the poor. God is so wise.

With all of our churches we have always put a high priority on ministry to the poor. In each church plant, before we would have our first Sunday morning service, we were already working among the poor in the community. I believe that in a very special way Jesus identifies with the poor, and the historical church has always understood this. That is why we opened up a free store with clothes and shoes, toys and school supplies for children. It is why we did small appliance repair for single mothers. We had a bus that we used to distribute groceries and clothing to housing projects.

We had taken the seats out and put in shelves and clothing racks. As soon as we pulled into the parking lot, folding tables would come out, laden with high quality free clothes; then the barbecues – before long there was a party with games for the kids, hotdogs, juice, prayer teams, and people who could simply listen as residents so often poured out their hearts. For years, and in many locations, I saw this scene repeat itself. People everywhere are meant for the joy of the Kingdom. I remember one Saturday morning as our strange looking purple bus pulled into a housing project, hearing a young boy shout out: "The mercy bus is coming! The mercy bus is coming!" We understood that the gospel is supposed to be good news to the poor, and good news travels fast. It means more than, "Now that you've received Jesus, I'll see you in heaven." Of course, while we were learning how to recognize and care for some of the needs of the poor in Canada, God was preparing us for the profoundly poor of the developing world.

One of the great adventures of my life occurred when I took a team to Russia in December/January of 1991-2. We arrived the day after Gorbachev announced the dissolution of the Soviet Union. We landed in a country in chaos. I will never forget the sight of old women sitting on the side of the road in St. Petersburg trying to sell such things as broken mirrors and pencil stubs. Accompanied by a military and police convoy for two hundred kilometers, we brought in two bus-loads of food and clothing to a married students' dormitory in the city. There were twelve hundred men women and children and all of them had been hungry for months. We set up the food and clothing in a gymnasium and invited students to enter in groups. I will always remember seeing a young woman so overcome at the sight of the food that she handed her infant to whomever happened to be standing beside her, leaned on a pillar and wept and wept. This time in Russia marked me deeply.

This was also a country that was spiritually starving; for seventy-four years preaching the gospel had been outlawed. We had been given thousands of illustrated booklets that told the story of the gospel in Russian. We would go on to the subway system and simply begin to hand them out. Every time as people realized what was being put in their hand, they called others to look too. I was kissed on my face, my neck, my hands; I was embraced, and I felt the tears of others pressed against my cheek. I do not know if I have ever known so many people to be so hungry for the gospel as at that time. Over the next four and a half years I went back to Russia several times a year. We sent containers of food to the starving nation. Whenever we sent a container, we arranged for someone from the West to be there to oversee the fair distribution of the food so that it got to the people who really needed it.

After a year, with so many people turning to Christ, I contacted some other leaders in North America to see if we could gather a team to plant a church in St. Petersburg. A few months later a team went over and a church was established that continues to this day. However, I think back to those days with mixed feelings. I simply did not understand the level of spiritual warfare that is involved in taking new territory, and I am sorry to say that our lack of concerted, mature intercession left our Russian team uncovered in a variety of ways. I am glad that the Lord lets us learn from every experience.

All of these experiences and many others prepared me for the next stage into which God was calling us.

IMPACT NATIONS

What is Impact Nations all about? It has been initiated from a deep conviction that the gospel that Jesus presented, the gospel of the Kingdom, is big and is powerful. It encompasses all aspects of life, both individual and communal. It touches health, economics, relationships, morality and politics. It is a gospel that brings "a living hope" (1 Pet. 1:3). The gospel of the Kingdom transforms every part of life. It is no more and no less "spiritual" to pray and see blind eyes opened than to get safe drinking water to a community that has never had it before. Jesus cares about all aspects of life and when we realize this and respond to this actively, everything changes.

The mission of Impact Nations is to build bridges of hope, healing and justice between those who are most vulnerable in the developing world, and people who are compelled by the love of Christ to help rescue lives. We bring tangible expressions of God's Kingdom and His compassion, both supernatural and practical. We work alongside nationals, seeking effective strategies for community transformation. We are deeply committed to working with local ministries, seeking to serve and encourage their dreams and visions for the people in their community.

As we do this bridge building, we recognize that each one has strengths to contribute to transformation. While we in the West often have more background in how to develop sustainable projects, how to plan and budget, and so on, the developing world without exception comes to us with the gift and lifestyle of faith that many of us can hardly imagine and from which we can certainly learn.

Throughout the year, Impact Nations takes teams of people from around the developed world into the developing world for two-week excursions that we call Journeys of Compassion. Since people come from so many nations and so many backgrounds, we begin each journey with a time of training and orientation. My goal is simple: for them to realize and then experience that God will use each one of them to release the Kingdom both supernaturally and naturally. For twelve days, each member engages in activities such as working in a mobile medical clinic where they help the medical staff, pray for the sick, or play with the children. They visit prisoners, go into schools, feed the hungry, and help with practical construction and farming projects. Every night we gather in villages to worship, present the good news of Jesus Christ, and have each member engage with the community in praying for the sick. This is life-changing for those involved, for both our team members and the villagers. Our commitment to go to the poor and the outcast takes us off the beaten track, into isolated villages in India where many will experience and hear the gospel of Jesus for the first time; to the urban slums of Manila; and to rural communities in other developing nations, where they have never before had a medical clinic.

Jesus said, "Heal the sick, cast out demons," so that is what we do. But He also said feed the hungry, give (clean, safe) water to the thirsty, visit the isolated and the stranger, provide clothing, visit the sick and the prisoner. Even more remarkably, He says that when we minister to these, the most poor and desperate, we are actively ministering to the one we love – Jesus. The gospel is practical and it is supernatural. We are committed to both presenting and living it as such.

We have now had hundreds of men, women and children join us in the front lines on a Journey of Compassion. Not only has everyone who has prayed for the sick personally seen God use them in healings and miracles, but again and again we have received letters, e-mails and phone calls telling us how their lives have been completely changed – not changed by Impact Nations, but changed by what I believe is intended to be normal Christianity, changed by being active participants in the Kingdom of God.

During the two weeks of a Journey of Compassion, we have the opportunity to work side by side with local ministries in the developing world, to work with the pastors and leaders, and to establish a relationship with the key leader and his team. Working together gives us all the opportunity to see if we can "do business together;" that is, to see if our values and our priorities are close enough that we can go to the next step. For us, the next step is usually establishing a project. We focus on projects because we believe the gospel of the Kingdom transforms communities in many ways, including economically; and once again, we firmly believe that the gospel is meant to be *"good news to the poor"* (Luke 4:18).

When we are moving in the rhythm of the Kingdom, it is surprising how quickly things advance. I remember our first mobile medical clinic in East Kenya. We had one suitcase of medicine and supplies and a lot of determination. I still remember as we went into the desert to a Muslim village, they had to chase away the camels from the shade of the only tree around, under which we set up our medical clinic. When we are willing to step out with the little bit that we have, God always seems to bless it. With this small beginning, He began to bring medical people from all over to help us. We have had doctors, nurses, pharmacists, lab technicians and emergency care workers come to us from Australia, the Netherlands, England, the United States and Canada.

•   •   •

One of the greatest health crises in the world is the problem of unsafe drinking water. Over 1.1 billion people on the planet have no access to safe water. Unsafe water kills more people than tuberculosis, malaria and AIDS combined. In 2006 we began our first clean water project in an isolated village in South India. We taught the locals how to build and install Bio-sand filters. From this small beginning, we have seen steady growth. We have helped provide safe water in two states in India, Zimbabwe and in twenty provinces in the Philippines. Not only do people receive safe drinking water, but also these projects provide full and part-time employment for over thirty people. As of this writing, we have provided safe water to over one hundred thousand people.

In some cases, sustainable projects can develop into social business. This is a term coined by the Nobel prize-winning economist, Mohammad Yunus. It refers to those businesses that are created for profit and to advance the social good. While greed is bad, Yunus points out that profit is good because it allows good works to go on and on. Impact Nations is working to develop social businesses wherever we see the opportunity. Our Bio-sand filter business in the Philippines is a prime example of how a growing business can impact entire regions, providing employment, working with governments and even partnering with other companies to provide an ever-increasing number of people with safe drinking water.

Because of our conviction that the Kingdom is meant to touch every part of life, not only are thousands of people receiving safe water, they are also receiving "living water." The Bio-sand filters take about an hour to install in peoples' homes. During this time our installers share the gospel and pray for the sick while setting up the new filter. In this way many people have experienced a very full expression of the Kingdom and have responded by giving their hearts to Jesus. There are now new believers gathering in homes in some very remote villages.

Working with our partners in the developing world, we have established sewing schools for widows and women at risk for those in the lowest castes in South India. This training has resulted in over eighty-five percent of the three hundred and sixty graduates now being fully self-supporting and in many cases supporting other family members. Although being a Christian was not a requirement for entrance into the schools, nor was becoming a Christian during the six-month training, every one of these women have given their lives to Christ. In fact, in the context of schooling they have seen remarkable miracles take place. One day a woman was sent home to die from the Hyderabad Hospital (a large, modern hospital). She had an inoperable brain tumor and was told there is nothing more that medical science could do for her. A relative heard about what was happening at the sewing school and brought the woman to these brand-new believers so that they would pray for her. The sewing school fasted for three days then prayed for the woman; she was totally healed and the Hyderabad hospital had no natural explanation. This is the Christian experience of these new believers in the sewing school. For them, this is normal Christianity. I sat under a tree one day listening as woman after woman gave remarkable testimonies of God's healing power in and through their lives.

We have come alongside our partners in Nicaragua, Uganda, Haiti, Philippines and India to help them provide food for children living in extreme poverty. Many of these children try to survive by scavenging in garbage dumps and begging. Through our Isaiah 58 Fast, we encourage people in the West to skip one meal a week, take that time to pray for the hungry of the world, and give what they would have spent on a meal. We also encourage small groups to give weekly to the Isaiah 58 Fast. Through this tangible expression of the love of God, we are now able to provide more than ten thousand meals a month.

We are also helping our partners in Africa by sending their representatives to a wonderful organization, Foundations For Farming, which has been getting remarkable results for over twenty-five years. By supporting them, Impact Nations is able to help a number of our partners to move from subsistence farming (growing just enough food to survive) to sustainable farming where there is enough to eat with crops left over which can be sold. We are delighted to see that the crop yield per acre is vastly increasing, providing more and better food for the orphans and poor school children whom our partners are working to help.

Our commitment to developing projects with our partners is finding new expressions every month. This includes providing electricity for poor rural schools so that the children do not have to bunch together where the light comes through the cracks in the wall, and so that evening classes can be provided, which helps keep children at risk in a safe environment. A simple thing like lights in a barrio in Nicaragua immediately stops the sexual assault that women and girls live with after dark. A six dollar treated mosquito net can provide anti-malarial protection for up to four children and is still the best known means of preventing malaria. As evidenced by the hundreds who walk great distances for help, conducting mobile medical clinics can have a major impact on community health. On numerous occasions we have seen that a mobile medical clinic can mean the difference between life and death.

Heidi Dunbar served as our Medical Director for a number of years. She set up the systems for going into remote villages with mobile medical clinics. So far, her groundwork has led to Impact Nations providing medical care for over thirty-eight thousand people who would otherwise be without. Heidi says:

> The medical life with Impact Nations is always an adventure that combines our "yes" to God's invitation, with our creativity, knowledge and flexibility. The very first medical clinic began under a tree in Eastern Kenya and it was inspired by a group of local nurses that said, "If you bring your medicine, we will take you to a nomadic tribe, who otherwise wouldn't have access to medicine or immunizations." We said, "Yes" and that was the beginning of something beyond our dreams. In response to the short-term nature of our medical missions, I have often been asked, "Isn't it better to teach a man to fish, than to give him a fish?" So one day I asked this question of God in relation to our clinics and I heard this reply, "Only if *I am asking you* to teach him to fish. If I give you fish to give, give it." God has used a small amount of medicine to impart hope to the hopeless, provide a venue for miraculous healing, open a door to long-term medical solutions, or to position us so we can literally save a life.
>
> Such was the case in Bulera, Uganda. Shortly after arriving to start our clinic I was handed a baby by her mother. Literally fighting for her life and only days old, this

infant was severely dehydrated, had a significant infection, was in respiratory distress, and likely hours from death. The family did not have money for transport, medicine or medical care. With the combined expertise of our team we were able to provide rehydration, treat the infection and nurse this baby back to life in our arms as we covered her in prayer and blessing. If we had arrived even one day later, it would have been too late for this baby. Out of a heart of 'Yes' and willingness to share the knowledge they have, God uses health professionals from around the world, to participate in rescuing lives that may have otherwise been lost.

• • •

So far, we have been able to help start over one hundred small businesses in India, Africa and Haiti. It is remarkable just how little financial capital is required to help someone start a small business that will change their life and impact their community. One of the most exciting approaches has been the development of micro-credit groups that provide very small business loans.

These micro-loans improve the individual's standard of living and help develop their businesses so that they can become self-sustaining and more profitable. Here is an example of what Impact Nations is doing in Mityana, Uganda. Working with our partners there, we helped set up and finance the Gracious Solutions Self Help Program. Those who want to receive a loan to start a small business begin by joining a GSSHP group, where individuals receive business training and consulting to improve their overall business skills. The GSSHP also provides a savings account for individuals in the community to better manage their income and plan for the future. Group lending improves accountability, responsibility, encouragement and empowerment to the individual's working together. This neighborly support system helps build relationships in the community and strengthen unity. As the loans are paid back, money is available for more people to start a life-changing business.

Furthermore, those managing the program for us in Mityana have pointed out that, as individual businesses grow, the community's economy follows suit and progressively develops. This continuation of business growth will attract more business entrepreneurs to the area. The Ugandan government will also be interested in investing in a fast developing community and offer their support.

The types of business that have been started are diverse, among them: small neighborhood grocery stores; a bridal tailoring business; a chapati business; piggeries; a carpentry business and a market gardening business. The possibilities are seemingly endless. What they all have in common is that in providing these loans, along with the accountability and coaching, these men and women are now able to be lifted out of deep poverty and into a life of greater dignity and hope. Surely, this is good news to the poor.

In 2010, while in Zambia, I was introduced to a very poor widow named Alice. She was raising eight orphans and her only asset was a bit of land and one milk cow. Alice used to walk to the town market every day with her two pails of milk in order to sell them and buy food for the orphans. However, it took Alice 3½ hours to walk from her home to the town market. By the time she arrived, the milk was sour because of the heat, and she was paid a lower price. It was easy in this case to see how we could make a difference, how the gospel could be good news to Alice. I simply purchased a bicycle for her – and everything changed. One month later I received an e-mail from her pastor telling me that now Alice only had to ride for forty-five minutes to the market, and that when she got there she could sell fresh milk at top price. Not only this, but she could now milk her cow twice a day and make two trips to the market. Her pastor excitedly told me that Alice's income had now tripled! Her pastor also told me that Alice had been secretly praying for a bicycle since 1987. Just how many prayers of the poor could be answered through us if only we would realize the possibilities?

• • •

The Impact Nations logo is a bridge that goes back and forth between East and West. Our motto is: "Rescuing Lives." The gospel of the Kingdom of God is for everyone, everywhere. We are aware of the great need in the West for God's Kingdom to advance. Each of us is made for the Kingdom. I believe that this is the stamp of the Creator God in every life. When we witness – even more, when we participate in – the activity of the Kingdom, something comes alive in us. This is the great and significant message that the Western church needs to embrace. There is a point of commonality that we have with all our neighbors: We all desire for our lives to make a difference. We live in an unprecedented era where what happens all over the world comes to us through the internet, our newspapers and television. I believe that the Holy Spirit has been stirring a greater awareness and longing for justice on the earth in this past decade. That is why we see more and more celebrities leveraging their fame and fortune for causes in Africa, South America and South East Asia.

Impact Nations is committed to bridging the desire of people in the West to make a difference, to the needs of the poor in the developing world. When neighbors gather in the living room and discover the great need that exists for medical care in a remote village in India, and that a mobile medical clinic can treat that village for as little as $300, people are both amazed and stirred in their hearts. A group of neighbors give, then and there, to make that medical clinic a reality. Because of the age that we live in, their gift becomes a medical clinic within just days. When people, whether Christians or not, start moving in the rhythm of the Kingdom, their hearts begin to be drawn toward the King and His cause.

When people see and participate in the activity of the Kingdom in the developing world, they usually take that new experience and begin to apply it in their world at home. As a direct result of Journeys of Compassion we have seen men and women release Kingdom activity in their own cities. Journey alumni are leading their friends into housing projects, soup kitchens and poor neighborhoods. They and their friends are engaging in empowered compassion where people not only receive food and clothing, but they also experience the supernatural healing power of the Kingdom of God.

Whether it is in a village in Africa, an urban slum in Manila, a housing project in North America, or in our own neighborhood, what I have learned, which my experience continues to reinforce, is that when we are moving in step with the King, there is a favor upon our lives that allows us to make a bigger difference and to make it faster than we ever thought was possible. Just how much could we accomplish, how much could we experience, how alive could we be, if we believed and embraced this truth?

As we step over our fears and doubts; as we fix our eyes on the One who says, "Follow Me, I am on the move"; as we embrace the joy of being who God has made us to be: sons and daughters empowered and commissioned to release God's Kingdom – then we discover that the impossible has become possible. When the Kingdom comes, everything changes.

**For more information on Impact Nations,
please visit www.impactnations.org**

ACKNOWLEDGEMENTS

The writing of any book involves many more people that just the author, including those who edit, encourage and critique. And then there are the men and women in the writer's life who have, over the years, been used by the Lord to help forge his life message.

I am grateful for all of you.

Thanks Sylvia for all the hours of reading, editing and making such helpful suggestions to more clearly express what was in my heart and mind. And thank you for your unwavering support through all these years of ministry.

Thank you Holly for reading the manuscript in its earliest form, with all its inconsistencies. Thanks for encouraging me to keep going. You helped me to see the path that this book needed to take.

Brad, thank you for believing in me and what I was trying to communicate enough to get behind this book.

Thank you Christina for reading and re-reading chapter after chapter. Your input shines through in the final manuscript.

And thank you to two spiritual fathers, who both have gone to join the "great cloud of witnesses" for teaching, correcting and guiding me on my journey of discovery with Jesus. Pastor Bob, you taught me to pray like no one else I ever knew. Your passion for the presence of God impacted and formed me. Dr. John, your knowledge and experience of releasing the reality and power of the Holy Spirit among God's people was a great inspiration. And thank you for all the times that you set aside just to be with a spiritual son. May I learn to be the kind of spiritual father that you were to me.

To my Impact Nations family around the world: little did I know when Impact began that God would form such strong and exciting bonds. Thanks Doug for your encouragement, your love of excellence and your love for the Kingdom. Thanks Paul and Johnny for believing in the vision, long before there was a track record of success. Heidi thank you for the dream of medical care in remote communities and the determination to bring it to pass. Greg and Cindy, thanks for your loyal friendship and dedicated service for all of these years. I am so glad to be on the journey with you both. Don, you planted the seed for this book through your encouragement, prophetic conviction and tangible investment. Sue, thank you for your continuous prayer support, prophetic insight and deep friendship. You truly are my sister. Thank you David for your courage and relentless trust in the goodness of God. Ministering together in the developing world has been a wonderful and rich adventure. Alan, thank you for letting iron sharpen iron, no matter what. You have a great love of truth that inspires me. Thank you for believing in me.

God has kindly given me spiritual children and I want to acknowledge their influence and encouragement in my life. It is wonderful to see them living out many of the principles expressed in this book. Thank you to Vijay and Neeraja in India; it is a joy to watch the Lord using you to raise up an army of disciples. Reg, I believe that your commitment to Christ and His Kingdom will change Haiti. Thank you for your faithfulness. Thank you Robert and Hannington for your examples of sacrifice and service. It is bearing much fruit in Uganda. Thank you Adam and Sarah, for the lives that you have chosen to live for Him. I am proud to be walking with you. Noah, thank you for your desire to keep learning more about His Kingdom, and to put what you learn into practice.

Not many men have a true best friend, one who is "closer than a brother." God gave me two of them. Bob and John, I miss you greatly and look forward to more adventures and more laughter together when one day we are re-united. Both of you were the best friends a man could ever have.

Lord Jesus, thank You for taking me, a young, confused, un-churched man all those years ago and reaching out and rescuing me. You have always been faithful, even when I haven't. Thank you for calling me to Your greater story. Thank you for writing Your purpose upon my life.

But especially, thank You for loving me ... and loving me ... and loving me.

FOR FURTHER READING

THE KINGDOM OF GOD

Bruner, Frederick Dale. *The Christbook: Matthew 1–12*. Grand Rapids: Eerdmans, 2004.

Jones, E. Stanley. *The Unshakable Kingdom and the Unchanging Person*. Nashville: Abingdon Press, 1972.

Lewis, C.S. *The Weight of Glory*. New York: HarperCollins, 1949/76.

Tozer, A. W. *The Knowledge of the Holy*. New York: Harper & Row, 1961.

Willard, Dallas. *The Divine Conspiracy*. New York: HarperCollins, 1998.

Williams, Don. *Signs, Wonders and the Kingdom of God*. Ann Arbor: Servant Books, 1989.

Wright, Christopher J. H. *The Mission of God*. Downers Grove: IVP, 2006.

Wright, Nicholas Thomas. *Surprised By Hope*. New York,: HarperCollins, 2008.

Yancey, Philip. *The Jesus I Never Knew*. Grand Rapids: Zondervan, 2002.

HEALING

Brasset, Bob. *All Things Are Possible*. Tonbridge, Kent, England: Sovereign World, 2004.

Bosworth, F. F. *Christ the Healer*. Grand Rapids: Fleming H. Revell, 1973.

Clark, Randy. *There Is More*. Mechanicsburg, PA: Global Awakening, 2006.

Keener, Craig. *Miracles: The Credibility of the New Testament Accounts*, 2 Vols. Grand Rapids: Baker, 2011.

Lake, John G. *The Complete Collection of His Life Teachings*. Tulsa, OK: Albury Publishing, 1999.

Osborn, T. L. *Healing the Sick*. Tulsa, OK: Harrison House, 1992.

Wigglesworth, Smith. *Smith Wigglesworth on Healing*. New Kensington, PA: Whitaker House, 1999.

GOD'S JUSTICE IN THE WORLD

Bornstein, David. *How to Change the World*. New York: Oxford University Press, 2007.

Claiborne, Shane. *The Irresistible Revolution*. Grand Rapids: Zondervan, 2006.

Haugen, Gary A. *Good News About Injustice*. Downers Grove: IVP, 1999.

Jersak, Brad. *Kissing the Leper: Seeing Jesus in the Least of These*. Abbotsford, BC: Fresh Wind Press, 2006.

King, Martin Luther. *A Testament of Hope*. New York: HarperCollins, 1886.

Lewis, Stephen. *Race Against Time*. Toronto: CBC, 2006.

Manning, Brennan. *Ruthless Trust*. New York: HarperCollins, 2002.

Meredith, Martin. *The Fate of Africa*. New York: PublicAffairs, 2005.

Mother Teresa. *No Greater Love*. Novato, CA: New World Library, 1989.

Smith, Danny. *Slavery Now and Then*. Eastbourne, England: Kingsway Communications, 2007.

Thurman, Howard. *Jesus and the Disinherited*. Boston: Beacon Press, 1976.

Wallis, Jim. *God's Politics*. New York: HarperCollins, 2005.

Wink, Walter. *The Powers That Be*. New York: Doubleday, 1998.

Wright, Nicholas Thomas. *Evil and the Justice of God*. Downers Grove: IVP, 2006.

Yoder, John Howard. *The Politics of Jesus*. Grand Rapids: Eerdmans, 1994.

Yunus, Muhammad. *Banker to the Poor*. New York: PublicAffairs, 2003.

62171590R00143

Made in the USA
Lexington, KY
31 March 2017